A GOURMET'S GUIDE TO
VENISON SAUSAGE
AND
COOKING VENISON

BY
JAMES A. LAHDE

WOODCOCK PRESS
ROCK, MICHIGAN

A Woodcock Press Publication

World rights reserved. No part of this publication may
be reproduced in any form nor may it be stored in a
retrieval system, transmitted, or otherwise copied for
public or private use without
prior written permission from the publisher.

First Edition - ©1997 by Woodcock Press
Second Edition - ©2002 by Woodcock Press
14636 Chapel Lane
Rock, Michigan, 49880.

Printed in the United States of America
ISSBN 0-9658554-2-2

TABLE OF CONTENTS

iv

ACKNOWLEDGEMENTS

Writing a cookbook on venison has truly been a labor of love mainly because it's the first time I was able to eat and enjoy the research. My love for cooking comes from Mom: a wonderful cook and a gracious teacher. My love for venison goes back to Dad who insisted on meticulous cleaning and utilizing of every scrap of game harvested. The interest in sausage also started many years ago helping Italian relatives make a variety of sausages. Most were eaten fresh but some found their way into saloon coolers, where they emerged, months later, as hard, yeast-covered salamis. Later, when attempts to duplicate the "old family recipe" in suburban basements and refrigerators resulted in constant failure, a passing hunger became a life-long quest to understand the mysteries of dry-cured sausage.

It took time to unravel these mysteries and appreciate the delicate nature of cooking venison. It also took a great deal of advice from friends and relatives to whom I would like to express my sincere appreciation. First, to my wife Virginia for her courage in sampling an endless variety of dishes. A special thanks goes to Lyle and Nancy Kirby, Adelaide DeJonge, Bob and Marlene Koski, Ted and Jacki Bartczek, and Bill Kury, for sharing recipes and objective criticism on dozens of "new" recipes. To sister Barb and husband Jerry, Elma Bakka, Michael Jetty, Ted Winkelbauer and son-in-law Ken for passing on their cherished family favorites. Last of all, a heart-felt appreciation to Uncle Jocko, Uncle Art and Aunt Mary who got me started on this long, wonderful, culinary crusade.

INTRODUCTION

V enison includes the meat of numerous species of deer: whitetail, mule deer, antelope, moose, caribou, elk as well as fallow and red deer. *A Gourmet's Guide To Venison Sausage And Cooking Venison* is a recipe book for anyone who enjoys hunting these marvelous animals and utilizing their venison to produce quality homemade sausage and exciting gourmet dishes.

The book is divided into three parts: 1) two chapter discussing the unique qualities of venison and the fundamentals of making sausage; 2) seven chapters on making venison sausage and jerky; and, five chapters on cooking various cuts of venison and making venison stock and pickle. Those chapters on sausage not only contain great recipes but advice and simplified techniques for making the more difficult semi-dry and dry-cured sausages. Such advice is especially valuable for those of us who lack fancy smokers and drying rooms. By using these in-house procedures it's easy to produce a high quality hard salami, luncheon meat, venison snack stick, or pepperoni.

The remaining five chapters are divided into such categories as slow roasting, broiling, frying and many other ways of preparing venison. Included are some old standards such as Venison Stroganoff, Venison Chili, Venison Stew and Venison Pasty. Those with an adventurous flair will find Venison Bagna Cauda, Paprika Snitzel Venison, Venison Galantine, Kidneys in Cream Sauce, Chicken-Fried Venison and numerous other creations truly delightful experiences.

Venison includes the meat of numerous species of deer: whitetail, antelope, moose, caribou, elk as well as fallow and red deer. *A Gourmet's Guide To Venison Sausage And Cooking Venison* is a recipe book for anyone who enjoys hunting these marvelous animals and utilizing their venison to produce quality homemade sausage and exciting gourmet dishes.

VENISON

Only in the last few years has the general public come to appreciate the value of venison not only for being lean and hormone free but for its wonderful flavor. For decades it was considered coarse fodder for rural poor. Much of its reputation was deserved given the fact immigrants to America had little contact with venison back in Europe where hunting and the cooking of wild game was a diversion practiced only by nobility. Consequently, the care needed in processing and cooking venison to realize its many benefits was a long time in coming. In addition, for decades our parents were bombarded with public-service ads pointing out the importance of only eating well-cooked meat. Such advice is good counsel for pork but destroys the fine texture and flavor of venison.

FIELD DRESSING VENISON

Thankfully, one need follow only a few simple rules to insure venison's fine, delicate texture and flavor is realized. First, insist on careful processing. In the field, be sure the meat is clean and cooled as rapidly as possible. If the animal is a male, in full rut, be especially careful not to transmit secretions on the back legs to any meat. Any meat contaminated with contents from the stomach pouch or intestines should be washed with cold water. If the smell remains, disregard that portion. Second, always carry several plastic bags for organs such as kidneys, liver, heart, tongue, and brain.

Often chefs will encase sausage or meat loaf in pig caul, a thin membrane encasing the intestines. Upon frying, the caul gives the sausage a wonderful brown, transparent sheen with darker streaks where veins of fat are caramelized. But pig caul is difficult to purchase. Venison caul can be utilized for the same purpose but must be collected during field dressing with a careful cut through the skin and muscle covering the intestines to expose the very thin membrane covering the intestines. With care the caul can be removed, rolled into a ball, and frozen until an appropriate sausage or loaf demands it use.

CUTS OF VENISON

To insure cleanliness throughout the butchering and packaging process it's best for the hunter to process his own animals. If this is not possible, insist the processor follow a few basic rules. One, ask that all fat and sinew be discarded with whitetail deer. Whitetail tallow, especially around the ribs, has a distinct taste and texture that is disagreeable to most people and should be replaced with pork fat where necessary. Also, request that fat smeared by cuts from a saw be removed. Since caribou and moose ribs have little or no fat and a generous amount of meat between the ribs, they are delicious and substitute for most any beef-rib recipe. In all cases, save the shanks and roast them as one would veal shanks. The amount of stew meat or venison burger you get from a shank is really not worth the effort whereas all the meat is excellent fare when braised until the meat falls from the bones.

A number of recipes in the following chapters recommend the use of venison tenderloin that lie alongside the backbone inside the animal's cavity, just in front of the back legs. On smaller animals like whitetail and antelope, be sure to remove the tenderloin as soon as possible. They have a tendency to dry and shrivel beyond recognition if not removed in the field. On whitetail the tenderloins are several inches wide and about eight inches long. They are much larger on moose, elk, and caribou. The extra work is worth the effort because they are most tender, savory, and deserving of special attention. Along with special handling in the field, they must be cooked quickly to preserve their tender, juicy qualities.

When tenderloin is not available for a recipe, substitute venison cutlets. Cutlets come from the backstrap or loin located along the backbone, above the ribs. Carefully removed, one backstrap on a mature whitetail will measure about 20-24 inches long. Some recipes suggest braising or roasting the whole loin, many others recommend sectioning the loin into one- or two-inch cutlets for quick frying, and a few counsel keeping the loin attached to the ribs for use as rib-racks.

There's an obvious difference in animal size that renders certain cuts available to moose, red deer, elk, and caribou that are not practical cuts on antelope, fallow, and whitetail. The tenderloins, tongue, shanks, and neck—even on the smaller animals—are worth the effort to obtain. On the larger animals only, the brisket and flank cuts are large enough to use in traditional flank and brisket recipes. The same is true with shoulder and chuck roasts. The neck on all species makes for a wonderful roast or can be shredded and used in any number of Mexican recipes or as barbecued venison (see p.88).

In all cases it's important to roast venison bones and then boil them slowly to extract the flavors for venison broth, a broth as good as any beef broth on the market. In some upscale restaurants it's chic to order venison leg bones roasted for their marrow (p.171 and 179).

CARIBOU VENISON
Special care must be taken with Caribou. Caribou meat is denser than whitetail or moose meat. It also maintains its redness beyond medium-rare. Therefore, a meat thermometer should be used whenever rare and medium-rare is desired.

SAUSAGE FUNDAMENTALS

Too often a person embarks upon a sausage-making career only to retire early when his or her hard work produces consistently poor results. First efforts with fresh sausage are usually successful. Fresh sausage is easy to make: simply mix quality seasoning with quality meat, let the mixture mature overnight, and, presto, a tasty treat. But for sausage addicts, the fascination comes with quality semi-dry and dry-cured sausages. Here is where problems arise. Dry sausage, salty sausage, bland sausage, and other poor products are common because so many recipes are incomplete. They fail to include the proper use of binders to retain moisture and correct techniques for curing, maturing, and aging sausage.

A salami recipe in a popular generic cookbook, for example, might simply contain a list of spices and a recommendations to dry the sausage for six or eight weeks. A more technical book might go to the opposite extreme with detailed recommendations on how to maintain a temperature of 100 degrees for eight hours, in a smoky, moist environment followed by suggestions to gradually increase the temperature to 180 degrees in a smoky, humid environment. Neither approach works for the home-sausage maker. One is too simple, the other near impossible to duplicate.

The main purpose of making sausages in this book is to clarify this confusion and simplify the process. To this end it's important to understand 1) sausage types and 2) sausage chemistry—or how salts, cures, binders, maturing, aging, and other factors affect sausage types. Once understood, a person should be able to take any basic recipe and enjoy it as fresh sausage, semi-dry sausage, or dry-cured sausage. For example, to convert a fresh sausage recipe into a small, moist venison snack stick simply add some additional salt, a little water, some corn syrup solids, nonfat dry milk, or soy protein powder. The addition of these products converts the Andouilli Venison Sausage—in the Semi-Dry Sausage Chapter—into a snack recipe for Andouilli Venison Sticks. The same technique could be used to convert a fresh sausage into a luncheon meat like an olive loaf. (See the introduction of each sausage chapter for additional information on converting recipes.)

Sausage Types

Sausages have been around for thousands of years with every culture having numerous variations on several basic types. Although there are hundreds, perhaps thousands of sausage recipes, most are classified as fresh, semi-dry, or dry-cured.

Fresh sausages include pork sausage and bratwurst. They are made of uncured, uncooked meat along with a variety of spices. They may be smoked or un-smoked and should be refrigerated and eaten within days.

Semi-dry sausages are represented by a host of products such as polish sausage, chaurice, andouilli, and kielbasa. Such products as olive loaf—often classified as luncheon meat—fall into this category as well. Many semi-dry sausages are usually heated in the smokehouse for cooking and partial aging. A special chapter is set aside for a group of semi-dry sausages, usually called summer sausage, that require special handling to develop their unique qualities. These products contain cures and are generally cooked and smoked, therefore, they have longer shelf lives than fresh sausage.

Dry-cured sausages generally differ from semi-dry sausages in the amount of salt they contain, their time spent aging, and the absence of cooking. Aging can last from one to six months depending on such factors as casing size, relative humidity, temperature, use of accelerators, air circulation, and whether or not they are smoked. Whereas five or six tablespoons of salt may be used for 10 pounds of semi-dry sausage, nine or 10 tablespoons might be recommended for 10 pounds of dry-cured sausage. Dry chorizo, pepperoni, salamini, and salami are classified as dry-cured products.

Sausage Chemistry

Following is a list of additives and techniques commonly used in making sausage. Included are recommendations and suggestions for their use. Additional suggestions are available at the beginning of each chapter.

Salt and Cures

Because many sausages are cooked or smoked at low temperatures for long periods of time, the risk of botulism is dramatically increased. Some bacteria thrive in these environments and their wastes may build to toxic levels. Over the centuries various types of cures evolved to help alleviate the risk, the most basic of which is plain salt, *sodium chloride. All the recipes in his book call for canning salt. Do not use table salt containing iodine.* Pure salt dissolves more completely than those containing additive. It acts as a binder, helps retain moisture, gives the meat a special flavor, and helps destroy disease organism that may be present before and during the aging process.

Cures containing sodium nitrite and sodium nitrate are used along with salt to flavor, maintain color, and help protect against disease organisms. Though not absolutely necessary for home use, they are recommended for both semi-dry and dry-cured sausages. This is especially true for dry-cured sausages that are aged for several weeks. Such products as Instacure, Prague Powders, and Legg Cure are examples of nitrite/nitrate cures. Suppliers of Legg Cure recommend four ounces of cure per 25 pounds of meat. This translates into 1 teaspoon per pound. Suppliers of Prague Powders recommend 1 teaspoon per 5 pounds of meat. Prague Powder #1 and Instacure #1 are used for semi-dry sausage while Prague Powder #2 and Instacure #2 are used for dry-cured sausage. Any butcher can provide a toll-free telephone number of companies carrying these products.

Morton Salt produces Morton Tender Quick® and Morton Sugar Cure® that are popular with many sausage makers because they combine both salt and cure. They contain salt, sugar, sodium nitrate and sodium nitrite. The recommended amount of Tender Quick® or Sugar Cure® for 10 pounds of meat is 1/2 cup or 1 1/2 teaspoon per pound. They also make a Smoke-Flavored Sugar Cure® they recommend for curing hams and bacons. All references in this book for Tender Quick® are for Morton Tender Quick® that can be purchased from most supermarkets. The company also offers a *Meat Curing Guide* that contains detailed steps along with salts, cures, and recipes for handling a variety of cuts. You can contact Morton Salt at Morton Salt, Consumer Affairs, 123 N. Wacker Drive, Chicago, Il 60660 or by telephone at 1 (312) 807-2693. Mail order information is available on their website: www.mortonsalt.com. Morton products are also available from Cumberland General Store: 1- (800) 334-4640.

Remember, Instacure, Prague Powders and Legg Cure help retain color and protect against botulism, but may not be needed in all cases. If a semi-dry sausage is to be eaten within days and color is not a concern, then cures are not necessary. But, if the product requires a maturing period, smoking at low temperatures or aging for several days, then cures are important. Also, as a rule, reduce the volume of salt by about half when adjusting dry-cured sausage recipes to semi-dry recipes. It may be helpful to change the type of cure as well. Prague Powder #1, for example, is used for semi-dry sausage, while Prague powder #2 and Instacure #2 are used for dry-cured sausages.

Cure Accelerators

Commercial sausage makers use cure accelerators to speed the curing and aging process. Accelerators also help reduce undesirable chemical by-products that result from nitrate decay. Sodium erythrobate and ascorbic acid—a powdered form of Vitamin C—are examples. Both are easily obtained from local pharmacies. One-half teaspoon of ascorbic acid is sufficient for 10 pounds of meat. The recommended ratio for sodium erythrobate is 7/8 ounce per 100 pounds.

Sugars

Sugar adds flavor, acts as curing agent, binding agent, and softens the hardness of salt. The distinct flavors of some semi-dry sausages are the result of bacterial fermentation in which sugars play an important role. Although plain table sugar (a complex sugar) works with fresh sausage, dextrose or corn sugar (simple sugars) are recommended for dry-cured and semi-dry sausage because bacteria digest simple sugars faster. Corn sugar is obtained from any outlet selling beer-making supplies.

Binders and Moisture Retention

Soy protein powder and lowfat dry milk help bind meat and fat together while retaining moisture during cooking or smoking. The result is a nice textured product with good slicing properties. Corn syrup solids add flavor as well. Liquid corn syrup can be substituted for corn syrup solids: 2 tablespoons of solids equal 1/4 cup of syrup. Many older recipes suggest using eggs and various sauces as binders. Cereals are used in some fresh sausages as binders as well. Rusk or toasted breadcrumbs can absorb four or five times their weight in moisture. The addition of a little bread or breadcrumbs soaked in milk also improves texture and flavor, generating a light, juicy product.

Disodium Phosphate is used commercially to retain moisture. One-quarter to 1/2 teaspoon of phosphate per pound of meat is the recommended dosage. Often, one teaspoon is combined with five ounces of soy protein powder to retain moisture in a 10-pound recipe. Disodium phosphate is available from Butchers and Packers, Detroit, Michigan: 1 (800) 521-3199.

Herbs and Spices

Herbs and spices add unique flavors to individual recipes. Most, like onion, garlic, mustard, fennel, and sage are by-products of plants. Salt, a mineral, serves a dual purpose in sausage both as a cure and spice. Providing a general list of seasoning for sausage is difficult because of the personal and cryptic nature of sausage making. For each popular sausage, such as chorizo, there are dozens of recipes, each with a different spice or two reflecting family or regional preferences. Since most commercial sausage makers jealously guard their recipes, one can only guess their ingredients. Plus, it's difficult to scale down large trade recipes for domestic use. There are a number of catalogs that offer pre-mixed packets of seasoning for most common sausages. Two popular sources are: The Sausage Maker, 26, Military Road, Buffalo, N.Y. 14207-2875 and Koch Supplies Inc.: www.kochsupplies.com. or 1 (800) 456-5624.

Monosodium glutamate (MSG) accentuates and enhances the flavor of spices as well as meat. MSG works proportionally with salt. The amount of MSG used should be two to five percent of the salt used. For home use, 1/4 teaspoon per pound of meat is recommended. MSG is found in most food markets under the name Accent.

Liquids-Cheese-Fruit

Water, hard liquor, beer, wine, and vinegar add moisture to sausage and are used primarily in fresh and semi-dry sausages to enhance flavor. Because of their high acid content, wine and vinegar are used in marinades as well as corning brines and pickles to help tenderize tough cuts. Ice chips are used in some cases as a water substitute. The ice keeps the meat and fat cool during mixing, preventing the fat from smearing.

Today, a number of sausage products are commercially available that feature cheese or dried fruit. One-half cup of cheese or fruit per pound of meat imparts flavor as well as a smooth, moist texture. The best cheeses to use are those imitation brands that will not melt under high temperatures.

Sour-Favor Enhancers

The Sausage Maker and Koch Supplies also sell sour-flavor enhancers that provide the tang to such products as summer sausage and hunter's sausage. Traditionally, their distinct flavor was obtained by allowing the meat and spice mix to mature at temperatures of 90 to 100 degrees for eight to 10 hours.

In the process, bacteria generated the desired sharpness. But for the home sausage maker to depend on the right bacteria to produce the right flavor can have spotty results.

Today, most sausage makers use encapsulated citric acid (ECA) or Fermento to insure a safe and tasty product. Fermento is a dairy product that requires a fermentation period of approximately one to two days at about 70 percent relative humidity and temperatures of 80 degrees to 90 degrees before cooking or smoking. Four to six ounces of Fermento are usually sufficient for 10 pounds of meat. Encapsulated citric acid does not require a fermentation period. Because it's heat sensitive, it should be added to cold meat just prior to casing. Approximately 1 tablespoon of ECA is sufficient for a five-pound recipe.

Smoking Venison

Smoking is an age-old tradition that was a side product of preserving meat by drying over fires. Today, wood smoke is applied mainly to enhance flavor. Liquid smoke—a concentrated by-product of smoke in liquid form—is used as a substitute for the smoking process. One tablespoon of liquid smoke per five pounds of meat is adequate to produce a smoky flavor. Or, some folks rub liquid smoke on the sausage just before cooking. All large food markets carry liquid smoke.

A major benefit smoke has over liquid smoke is the visual appearance of the finished product. The rich, distinctive color of a well-smoked sausage cannot be duplicated with liquid smoke. A hot smoke—involving temperatures usually over 150 degrees for a period of two to three hours—is sufficient to smoke and cook small sausages. Cold smoking, with temperatures under 100 degrees imparts the smoky flavor but is not sufficient to cook the meat and takes longer to produce the same smoky flavor as a hot smoke.

The problem with many recipes calling for hot smoking is that temperatures of home smokers cannot be effectively controlled. The typical recipe for a quality summer sausage, for example, calls for maintaining smoke house temperature at 100 degrees for eight to 10 hours, then, slowly raising the temperature until an inside temperature of 155 degrees is achieved. This process is very important. The eight to 10 hours at 100 degrees is a fermentation period that generates a characteristic flavor and the low temperature reduces moisture loss. Maintaining 100 degrees for eight to 10 hours then slowly increasing the temperature to 155 degrees is difficult to accomplish in the backyard smoker.

With small volumes of sausage these problems are solved by 1) cooking the sausage slowly in the kitchen oven at temperatures no higher than 170-180 degrees until an inside temperature of 155 degrees is reached; 2) maintaining a high moisture level in the oven with a pan of water and periodic spraying; 3) cooling the sausage down quickly by spraying with cold water; and, 4) using liquid smoke or a cold smoke to achieve the smoky taste and color desired.

Casings

Natural and synthetic casings are purchased at most butcher shops or companies that service meat markets. Synthetic casing are sold by the millimeter (mm) and range from 20-50mm. Synthetic, fibrous casings come in several colors but are not eatable. Protein-lined fibrous casings cling to meat and are often used for aging sausage. Collagen casings are clear, tender, and eatable synthetic casings.

Natural casings come packed in salt and should be rinsed, both inside and out with cold water. This is especially true for pig and beef casings. Sheep casings are considered small (20-28mm); hog casing, medium (28-40mm); and, beef casings, large (40-50mm). Some sausage makers turn the casings inside out to expose the strands of fibrous fat that line one side of the casings before stuffing.

Cutting a section of cheesecloth three inches wider and at least twice the circumference of the planned sausage produces cheesecloth casings. Wet the cheesecloth, then hand dip into melted lard and spread out on a tray. Form the sausage near one edge and roll it up to enclose the meat completely. Tie the sausage at one end, then wrap a spiral of string around the sausage from one end to the other. Finish by tying the other end, then smear with lard once again.

A number of not-so-common products are available for those willing to search and experiment. Pig caul—the membranous lining covering a pig's intestines—is occasionally used in upscale restaurants to wrap sausage meats (p.6) and is available if one knows a butcher of pigs. As a substitute, use the caul from members of the deer family. Skin from the neck or breast of geese, turkeys, and chickens works especially well for a sausage that's to be roasted.

A deer's stomach pouch, like the stomach pouch of sheep used to make haggis, might be used as a container for sausage (see Venison Haggis, p.169). Start by removing any glands and loose skin from the outside. Next, wash the pouch several times, turn it inside out, and then plunge into boiling water for 30 seconds. The inside lining is composed of small finger-like projections that are best removed by scraping with the edge of a large spoon. The end result is a soft, pliable pouch that—from a small whitetail—will hold approximately 1 1/2 quarts of stuffing.

Protecting Against Trichinosis

Trichinosis is a muscular disease caused by the parasitic trichina worm common to pork. The worm is killed by cooking pork to a temperature of 155 degrees or by freezing. Well spaced pieces of pork less than six inches thick should be held for 20 days at five degrees, 10 days at minus 10 degrees, and six days at minus 20 degrees.

Fat

Fat is important to any sausage. It acts as a marinade inside the casing where diverse ingredients are blended and intensified providing the savory qualities of so many sausages, especially semi-dry varieties. Too little fat results in a rather dry, tough sausage. Pork fat is used most often with beef combinations useful in some recipes. The fat of choice is hard back fat from the pig which, like pig caul, is not easy to come by today. Though not as heat tolerant as hard back fat, bacon and the trimmings from pork butts are common substitutes with many home-sausage makers.

In no case should whitetail fat be used. It does not mix well with spices and has a distinct, unappetizing flavor. As a rule, the proportion of fat to lean meat in venison sausage should be between a third and a half. In bologna, wieners, pickle loafs, and other fine-textured recipes containing soy protein powder and/or lowfat dry milk, a ratio as high as 80 percent venison to 20 percent pork is justified. This same ratio is appropriate for summer sausage recipes. A ratio of one-third pork, one-third venison, and one-third pork fat is recommended for a rich sausage.

Maturing Sausage

The meats, spices, fats, and other ingredients found in all sausage need time to mature. This maturing or resting period, blends the flavors, marries the spices, and helps develop proper texture. Because fresh sausage lacks sufficient cures, they should mature only overnight in the refrigerator. Resting periods for semi-dry sausages vary considerably. Some mature in the refrigerator overnight and some need warm, humid environments for several days to mature and ferment. Some develop their flavor over hours of slow cooking or slow smoking. Many dry-cured sausage recipes recommend a maturation period of one to two days at 70 degrees before aging at lower temperatures of 40-50 degrees and high humilities of 60-70 percent for weeks or months. The volume of cures and salts in these recipes justify the exposure to warm temperature for short periods of time. See chapters on Semi-Dry and Dry-Cured Sausage for additional information on maturing.

Aging Sausage

Whereas maturing is a *short* resting period to develop flavor, aging is a *long* curing period to develop flavor and texture. In dry-cured sausages, extended curing also takes the place of cooking. During this time, water evaporates and harmful organisms are destroyed by salt and nitrite cures thereby preserving the meat and eliminating the need for cooking. In addition, the meat marinates and ferments in the spiced oils and water allowing flavors to coalesce, mellow and permeate the fibers. In the process, a sausage will lose approximately 30 percent its green or original weight.

Extending aging requires controlled humidity and temperature. Proper humidity (abut 60 percent) permits the sausage to dry slowly, from the inside out. In a dry environment, the exterior dries too quickly forming a hard rind. This rind acts as a protective covering preventing further evaporation, resulting in a poor tasting sausage that's hard on the outside and punky on the inside. See chapter on Dry-Cured Sausage for additional information on aging.

Cooking Sausage

In the cooking process there is little practical difference between moose, caribou, elk, and whitetail from the standpoint of flavor and texture. It's generally agreed that moose is the most like beef but all—cooked properly are excellent. There are some minor differences that exist with Caribou. Caribou has denser meat containing less moisture so, while just as tasty and tender, it's more difficult to grind and requires the addition of oils and fats in cooking to achieve a moist product. A meat loaf make only of caribou meat will be dry if pork fat or oil is not added. Also, at temperatures of 135 degrees for rare or 140 degrees for medium-rare, caribou will have a more reddish tint to the meat, giving the impression it's more rare than it actually is, which reinforces the importance of using a reliable meat thermometer.

To retain moisture and flavor, cook fresh sausage in a heavy skillet. Add a little water, cover and simmer until cooked through, drain and brown lightly. Some fresh, bulk sausage lacking binders are best baked or broiled because they have a tendency to fall apart when turned during frying. A little water with a small sausage patty cooked in the microwave works well to quickly steam-cook the sausage.

Most semi-dry sausages are cooked or smoked as part of their preparation so they need only be baked, poached, broiled, or grilled to heat and crisp the casing. Poaching is best done gradually at low temperatures (160-180 degrees) until the inside temperatures reaches 155 degrees so the moisture stays in the sausage. Do not prick the sausage during poaching and allow the sausage to cool slightly before eating to permit the fibers to absorb the juices. Sausage cooked too long in soups or stews can lose their flavor. To preserve their individual flavors, add the cooked sausage just prior to serving.

Dry-cured sausages are normally uncooked, sliced thin and served as appetizers, as luncheon meats, or on pizzas. In most cases, cooking a partially aged dry-cured sausage produces a totally different sausage. For example, an Endini Salami (p.56) was boiled for 30 minutes after it had aged for four weeks. Served warm, the sausage was excellent: moist and flavorful with good color and a long, sweet finish totally different than the dried version.

FRESH SAUSAGE

Fresh Sausage includes a great variety of bulk, skinless, and cased products including the English Cumberland and Lageneghe, the French Toulouse, the Italian Salamelle, the spiced Merquez from North North Africa, and the Lap Cheong from China. Technically, fresh sausage does not contain enough curing agents to "survive" outside the refrigerator for more than several hours and in the refrigerator for more than a week. Some bockwursts, that contain eggs, milk, and a few spices are highly perishable.

Any sausage when first made may be enjoyed fresh—even a Genoa Salami—but not all the ingredients that go into a hard salami are needed to enjoy it fresh and are, therefore, a waste of time and money to include. On the other hand, the addition of a few items can have wonderful results. For example, a lighter, softer product is produced with the addition of more fat or grain such as cereal, rusk, or breadcrumbs. Toasted breadcrumbs can absorb four to five times their weight in moisture and will keep that moisture locked in the sausage while cooking.

It's also important for a fresh sausage—like all mixtures of meat and spices—to rest or mature in a refrigerator at least overnight to develop its full flavor. To retain moisture and flavor while cooking a fresh sausage, use a heavy skillet with a little water and simmer until cooked through, then drain and brown quickly. A little water and a small sausage patty cooked at high power in the microwave also works well.

By adding more salt, a nitrite cure, and some binder, it's possible to create a semi-dry or dry-cured sausage from most any fresh sausage recipe.

There are two theories on boiling or poaching fresh sausage. Some, like Cudighi (p.30), are excellent simmered—without pricking—at low temperatures (170°-180°) until the inside temperature registers 155 degree on a meat thermometer, then quickly cooled to prevent fat and spices from leaching out. Some folks like to brown their sausage then steep the sausage in a simmering beer/water solution to be consumed, at random, during an afternoon of recreation but, as a rule, such extended cooking can rob the sausage of moisture and taste.

Maintaining Moisture
Coarse ground meat will retain more moisture and fat than finely ground meat.

Cudighi Sandwich
Toasted Italian rolls, fried onions, pizza sauce, and a broiled patty of cudighi covered with Mozzarella cheese.

Chorizo Sausage

Chorizo is a coarse, spicy, garlic sausage with its origin in Spain that's common in the South and Southwest. This is a very loose sausage that's often scrambled with eggs, browned with potatoes, or served on tortilla shells with crisp lettuce and melted cheese. It is also a wonderful addition to Mexican pizza.

- -

3/4 # venison	1 tsp. hot red pepper	1/3 cup vinegar
3/4 # pork	1/4 tsp. coriander	1/8 tsp. cloves
2 tbsp. paprika	1/2 tsp. cinnamon	1/8 tsp. ginger
1 heaping tsp. salt	1 tsp. oregano	1/8 tsp. nutmeg
1/4 tsp. black pepper	3 cloves minced garlic	

- -

Grind meat through a 1/4" plate. Add all ingredients and mix well. Store in cooler for 24 hours to permit meat and spice mixture to mature. Use in bulk or stuff into 35 mm (2") hog casings. (The addition of 1/2 cup breadcrumbs will bind the sausage and make a better product for grilling.)

Red Hot Breakfast Sausage

Don't stuff all this sausage in casings. A small patty popped in the microwave makes a wonderful snack. You may decide to make extra for those special Mexican dishes. For this recipe, it's best to grind the anise seeds and red pepper flakes rather than use powdered forms.

- -

2 1/2 # venison	2 tbsp. corn syrup solids*
2 1/2 # pork	1/2 tsp. allspice
5 tsp. sugar	2 tbsp. paprika
4 1/2 tbsp. salt	2 1/2 tsp. anise seeds
1 tbsp. red pepper	cure (optional)**

> In fresh sausage, nitrite cures are used to preserve the pink color of the meat.

- -

*One-quarter cup liquid corn syrup is a substitute for corn syrup solids
**Volume of cure depends on type of cure used. See p. 10

Grind meat through a 1/4" plate. Mix all ingredients with meat. Shape into patties or stuff into 35mm (2") casings. To retain moisture and flavor while cooking a fresh sausage, use a heavy skillet with a little water and simmer until cooked through, then drain and brown quickly.

Fennel Sausage

Fennel sausage is popular in many recipes from southern Italy. A high pork content maintains the necessary fat needed to sweeten the meat, mature the spices, and produce a juicy product.

- -

2 # venison	1/2 cup sugar
3 # pork	1 1/2 tsp. ground red pepper
1 cup water	1 1/2 tsp. ground caraway seed
2 1/2 tbsp. salt	1 tsp. garlic powder
1/2 tbsp. ground fennel	cure (optional)*

- -

*Volume of cure depends on type of cure used. See p.10

Grind meat through a 1/4" plate. Mix all ingredients with meat. Make into patties or stuff into 35mm (2") casings. To retain moisture and flavor while cooking a fresh sausage, use a heavy skillet with a little water and simmer until cooked through, then drain and brown quickly.

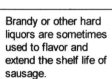

Brandy or other hard liquors are sometimes used to flavor and extend the shelf life of sausage.

Venison Sauscisses

Sauscisses is a Creole sausage traditionally made with beef, veal, and pork but venison works well as a beef substitute. Sauscisses is often pan fried for breakfast, grilled as a side dish to red beans and rice, to flavor gumbo, or add zest in a sandwich

- -

2 # venison	1 tbsp. black pepper	3 bay leaves
3 # pork	1 tsp. thyme	1 tsp. marjoram
1 # veal	1/2 tsp. cloves	1/2 tsp. allspice
1 clove minced garlic	1/2 tsp. mace	1 tbsp. cayenne
3 tbsp. salt	1/2 tsp. nutmeg	cure (optional)*
3 large onions, minced		

- -

*Volume of cure depends on type of cure used. See p.10

Grind meat through a 1/4" plate. Add onions and spices. Mix thoroughly. Mature overnight to enhance the flavor. Use in bulk or stuff into medium 35mm (2") casings. To retain moisture and flavor while cooking a fresh sausage, use a heavy skillet with a little water and simmer until cooked through, then drain and brown quickly.

Pistachio Sausage

Make pistachio sausage into patties and fry, broil, or stuff into casings and poach. Once poached, serve warm, cold, or sliced and browned in a bit of butter along with some onions.

- -

1 # venison	1 clove garlic
1 # pork	1/4 tsp. paprika
1 # pork fat	1/4 tsp. allspice
1 1/2 tbsp. salt	1/4 tsp. thyme
1 tbsp. cayenne	1/4 cup brandy
1/2 tsp. white pepper	3/4 tsp. sugar
3 large onions, minced	cure (optional)*

- -

*Volume of cure depends on type of cure used. See p.10

Grind meat through a 1/4" plate. Add all other ingredients and mix thoroughly. Use as bulk sausage or stuff into medium 35mm (2") casings. Mature in cool environment for two days.

> Try simmering sausage in beef bouillon and wine for about 30 minutes.

Venison Cudighi

Cudighi (pronounced good-a-gee) is a fresh Italian sausage that's fried, broiled as a patty, or stuffed into casings and poached. It's popular in Michigan's Upper Peninsula where it's found fresh, on pizza, or in cudighi sandwiches (p.24). Combine a bit of breadcrumbs soaked in a little milk, some chopped, dried apricots—or other dried fruit—with cudighi to make superb meatballs.

3 # venison	1/2 tsp. mace	3 tbsp. sugar
7 # pork	1/4 tsp. cinnamon	2 cloves minced garlic
6 tbsp. salt	1/2 tsp. ground cloves	2 tsp. black pepper
1 tsp. ground nutmeg	1/2 cup dry red wine	cure (optional)*

*Volume of cure depends on type of cure used. See p.10

Add garlic to wine. Grind meat through 3/8" plate. Combine all ingredients into meat and mix well. Shape into patties or stuff into 35mm (2") casings. Refrigerate for two days. Poached cudighi is excellent. Simmer in hot water (about 180°) until inside temperature reaches 155°. Then cool immediately under cold water.

Venison Potato Sausage

Wherever pockets of Scandinavians live, uncounted potato-sausage addicts are found. Like the Cornish pasty, churches and community organizations use this simple recipe as a sure-fire fund-raiser.

- -

2 # venison	1/4 cup salt
3 # pork	1 tbsp. black pepper
1 cup chopped onions	1/4 cup Accent
7 1/2 # cubed potatoes	

- -

Grind pork, venison, onions, and potatoes through 3/8" plate. Add spices and mix well. Stuff into 35mm (2") hog casings very loosely. Cover with water until ready to bake. Bake, uncovered in heavy skillet with a little olive oil at 350° for 1 hour or until casings are golden brown and crispy. Spray with water the last 15 minutes to help crisp the sausage.

Potatoes will turn black unless the sausage is cooked immediately, parboiled and frozen, submerged in water, or stabilized with whitening prior to grinding.

Venison Liver Sausage

Those who like Braunschweiger will thoroughly enjoy this coarse liver sausage. Leftover or loose sausage quickly fried alongside scrambled eggs and served over toast is a real delight.

- -

1 1/2 # venison liver	2 tbsp. nonfat dry milk
1 large onion	1/4 cup corn syrup
1/2 cup butter	1 cup chopped raisins
2 cups cooked, chilled rice	1/2 tsp. ginger
4 eggs	1 tsp. white pepper
1 1/2 tbsp. salt	

> Since the mixture is so fluid, a pastry bag may work just as well as a sausage press.

- -

Blanch liver in boiling water for 3 minutes. Grind liver and onions through 1/4" plate or process in food processor. Add all other ingredients and mix well—mixture will be fluid. Stuff, *loosely*, into 40mm (3") casings. Tie into 6" lengths. Simmer—*do not boil*—for 30 minutes. Prick with needle during cooking to release air pressure. Cool quickly and store in refrigerator or freeze. When ready to serve, brown in oven or frying pan.

Spicy Italian Sausage

Serve this spicy, tangy sausage for breakfast, lunch, or dinner. Because of its pepperoni flavor, it works well on pizza, in Italian sandwiches, or Mexican dishes.

- -

2 # venison	1 tbsp. grated Parmesan cheese
2 # pork	1 1/2 tsp. black pepper
1 # bacon	1 tsp. sugar
2 1/2 tbsp. salt	1/2 cup red wine
5 tsp. ground fennel	cure (optional)*
1 tbsp. red pepper	

- -

*Volume of cure depends on type of cure used. See p.10

Grind meat through 1/4" plate. Mix all ingredients with meat. Stuff into medium, 35mm (2") hog casings. Refrigerate overnight. Steam over medium-low heat in heavy skillet with a little olive oil and 2 tablespoons of water for 5 minutes. Raise temperature to medium-high and brown quickly.

English Breakfast Sausage

This recipe has very little salt and no pepper. Fresh bread soaked in milk, with the excess milk squeezed out by hand, is a good substitute for breadcrumbs and water. The encapsulated citric acid provides a mild tang that can be increased or decreased according to taste.

- -

1 # venison	1/4 tsp. marjoram
1 # pork	1/2 tsp. sage
1/2 # bacon	1 tsp. pepper
2 tsp. salt	1/4 tsp. thyme
1/2 cup breadcrumbs	1/2 tsp. ECA*
1 cup water	

- -

*ECA: Encapsulated citric acid – mix with cold meat prior to stuffing. See p. 14

Grind meat through 1/4" plate. Mix all ingredients with cold meat—ECA last. Stuff into small 20-25mm sheep casing (1"), collagen casings, or maintain as bulk sausage. Mature overnight in refrigerator. Steam for several minutes, then brown in hot olive oil and butter.

> Fresh bread soaked in milk gives the sausage a lighter, softer texture similar to well-made meatballs.

Venison Cherry Patties

Today there's a great variety of seasoned bread stuffing and dried fruit that will enhance old recipes. Seasoned breadcrumbs help bind moisture and add flavor while dried fruit provides color, texture, and additional flavor.

- -

1 # venison	6 tbsp. chopped dried cherries*
6 chopped, green onions	1/2 cup corn bread stuffing mix
2 tsp. sage	2 tbsp. butter
1 tsp. pepper	1/2 tsp. sage
1 tsp. salt	1 cup red wine

- -

*Dried apricots, apples, or other fruit will also work.

Grind meat through 1/4" plate. Crumble corn bread stuffing mix. Mix all ingredients, except butter, 1 cup red wine, and 1/2 teaspoon sage. Mature overnight in refrigerator. Shape into patties. Cook patties in butter, then remove from pan. Add wine and 1/2 teaspoon sage to skillet and simmer to 1/2 volume or until sauce coats a spoon. Pour sauce over patties and serve hot.

Venison Cervelas

Cervelas sausage is found on menus all down the east side of France as well as French areas in Canada and Newfoundland. Traditionally, cervelas is served with potato salad or sauerkraut.

- -

1/2 # venison	1/2 clove minced garlic
1 # pork	2 shallots, chopped
1/2 # fat pork or bacon	1/2 tsp. black pepper
2 tbsp. salt	cure*

- -

*Volume of cure depends on type of cure used. See p.10

Chop bacon into small 1/4" squares. Grind venison and pork through 1/4" plate. Combine all ingredients and stuff into medium 30mm (1 1/2") casings. Prior to simmering in near boiling water or wine, cerveles sausage is usually hung to mature for several days in a cool place (50-60°). Then, it may also be lightly smoked or brined for three days in a salt brine or vinegar pickle before cooking.

Venison BBQ Links

Hot, smoky, spicy barbecue links should be served on crusty Italian rolls with plenty of barbecue sauce and caramelized onions.

- -

1 1/2 # venison	2 tbsp. minced garlic
1 # pork loin	2 tsp. cayenne powder
1/2 # fat pork or bacon	1/2 tsp. sage
1 1/2 tbsp. salt	1/4 tsp. each allspice, cloves, coriander,
1 tbsp. pepper	cinnamon, and cardamom
2 tsp. sugar	1 1/2 tbsp. paprika
1 tsp marjoram	

- -

Grind venison, fat, and pork through 3/8" plate. Combine all ingredients, mix well and stuff into medium 35mm (2") casings. Mature overnight in refrigerator. Hot smoke until inside temperature is 155° or bake in moist oven at low temperature (180°) until inside temperature is 155°. Cold smoke for 4 hours.

Venison Milano Sausage

The essence of many mild Italian sausages comes not only from herbs and spices but from the subtle aroma of wines, vegetables, and fruits. Dried raisins, apricots, or prunes are good substitutes for the dried tomatoes listed below.

---

1 # venison	1 tbsp. basil
2 # pork butt	1/2 cup red wine
1 # bacon or hard back fat	1/2 tbsp. oregano
1/2 cup dried tomatoes	1/4 tsp. allspice
2 tsp. salt	1/4 tsp. thyme
1/2 tbsp. pepper	

Soak tomatoes in olive oil or wine. Freeze bacon in strips. Grind venison, pork butt, and tomatoes through 3/8" plate. Grind bacon strips through 1/4" plate. Combine all ingredients and mix well. Stuff into medium, 35mm (2") hog casings. Refrigerate overnight. Steam over medium-low heat in heavy skillet with a little olive oil and 2 tablespoons of water for 5 minutes. Raise temperature to medium-high and brown quickly.

SEMI-DRY SAUSAGE

Compared to fresh sausage, semi-dry sausage has a longer shelf life with unique individual characteristics that come with longer aging and smoking. Semi-dry sausages are semi-soft with good keeping qualities due to their lactic acid fermentation. Think of a crisp Polish sausage, bursting with flavor, hot off the grill or a warm ring bologna topped with a dollop of mustard. Is there anything better? The unique qualities of each are developed during a lengthy process that may include slow cooking, smoking, fermenting, and aging. Because each process is long and conditions perfect for undesirable bacterial growth, precautions must be taken to reduce the risk of food poisoning while enhancing flavors and retaining water and fat.

Adding binders to help retain moisture and generate a nice texture solves part of the moisture problem. Adding curing agents to prevent bacterial growth, adding cure accelerators to speed up aging, by careful cooking, and prudent refrigeration, reduces health risks. A simple in-house procedure for cooking a semi-dry sausage is to:

1) Set the oven at 170-180 degrees and heat the sausage slowly until inside temperature reaches 155 degrees;
2) Maintain a high moisture level in the oven by including a pan of water and periodic spraying;

3) Cool the sausage down quickly under a cold-water spray or ice bath; and,

4) Cold smoke for a minimum of 2 hours to achieve the smoky taste and color. Liquid smoke provides adequate taste but will not give a rich color to the casing.

The use of binders and slow, moist cooking helps maintain moisture but the type and volume of fat is also an important factor. Since venison lacks fat—or in the case of whitetail, the fat is undesirable—it's often necessary to add pork or beef fat to sausage. Beef fat is used to a limited degree in some summer sausages and kosher salamis but hard fat back from hogs is preferred. Hard fat back is flavorful and has a higher melting point than other fats. Bacon or the trimmings from pork putts are good alternatives to hard fat back. For a rich sausage use 1/3 venison, 1/3 pork, and 1/3 pork fat.

Remember, it's easy to convert one type sausage to another. For example, fresh cudighi (p.30) is easily converted to Endini Salami (p.66) with the proportional addition of corn syrup solids, dextrose, a cure, and more salt to the fresh cudighi recipe. The result is then placed in a cool place with high relative humidity (the bottom drawer in the refrigerator, for example) and left to dry slowly for several weeks or months, depending on the size of the casing.

Venison Polish Sausage

Marjoram is distinctive in this juicy sausage so be careful with the amount used. The sausage is very good smoked, un-smoked, or flavored with liquid smoke.

2 # venison	1 tbsp. sugar	3 tbsp. salt
2 # pork	1/2 tbsp. black pepper	1/2 tsp. marjoram
1 # bacon or hard fat back	1 tbsp. garlic powder	cure*
2 cups water	5 tbsp. liquid smoke (optional)	

*Volume of cure depends on type of cure used. See p.10

Chill meat thoroughly. Grind meat through 1/4" plate. Add spices. Mix well. Refrigerate overnight. Stuff into medium 35 mm (2") hog casings. Place cake pan filled with water in bottom of oven. Bake sausage in 170°-190° oven for about 4 hours or until inside temperature is 155°. Spray oven occasionally. Cool sausage down immediately with cold water. Cold smoke if desired.

When using liquid smoke, apply it just prior to cooking the sausage.

Creole Venison Sausage

Traditional Creole sausage is spicy—often hot—and enjoyed both fresh and semi-dried. It's often pan fried for breakfast, grilled as a side dish to red beans and rice, to flavor gumbo, or add zest in a sandwich.

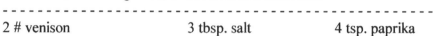

2 # venison	3 tbsp. salt	4 tsp. paprika
3 # pork	2 tsp. garlic powder	cure*
1/2 # bacon or hard fat back	1/2 tsp. ground bay leaves	
2 tsp. cayenne	5 tbsp. liquid smoke (optional)	
1/4 tsp. chili pepper	1/2 tsp. sugar	

*Volume of cure depends on type of cure used. See p.10

Chill meat thoroughly. Grind meat through 1/4" plate. Add spices. Mix well. Refrigerate overnight. Stuff into medium 35 mm (2") hog casings. Place cake pan filled with water in bottom of oven. Bake sausage in 170°-190° oven for about 4 hours or until inside temperature is 155°. Spray oven occasionally. Cool sausage down immediately with cold water. Cold smoke if desired.

Chaurice Venison Sausage

Chaurice is the Creole version of chorizo, a coarse, spicy-hot Mexican sausage eaten both fresh or smoked as a semi-dry sausage. Re-hydrated onions can be substituted but lack the moisture of fresh onions.

2 # venison	3 tsp. red pepper	1/2 tsp. allspice
2 # pork	2 cups chopped onion	2 tsp. thyme
1 # bacon or hard fat back	2 tbsp. black pepper	4 tsp. garlic
2 1/2 tbsp. salt	5 tbsp. fresh parsley	cure*
3 whole bay leaves, ground		

*Volume of cure depends on type of cure used. See p.10

Chill meat thoroughly. Grind meat through 1/4" plate. Add spices. Mix well. Refrigerate overnight. Stuff into medium 35 mm hog casings. Place cake pan filled with water in bottom of oven. Bake sausage in 170°-190° oven for about 4 hours or until inside temperature is 155°. Spray oven occasionally. Cool sausage down immediately with cold water. Chaurice is usually eaten fresh but is sometimes lightly smoked.

Andouilli Venison Sausage

Andouilli is a Cajun sausage with European origins in France and Germany. Traditionally it's cold smoked to give it a rich smoky flavor. Like Creole sausage, it's used to season gumbo soup, as an appetizer, or side dish with red beans and rice. For a hotter sausage, use more cayenne.

- -

2 # venison	1/8 tsp. cayenne	1/2 tsp. black pepper
2 # pork	1/8 tsp. chili powder	1/4 tsp. ground bay leaves
1 # bacon or hard fat back	1/8 tsp. mace	1/4 tsp. sage
2 tbsp. salt	1/8 tsp. allspice	cure*
3 1/2 tbsp. garlic	1/2 tsp. paprika	

Traditionally, tripe, chitterlings, belly pork and calf mesentery were the main ingredients in andouilli.

- -

*Volume of cure depends on type of cure used. See p.10

Chill meat thoroughly. Grind meat through 1/4" plate. Add spices. Mix well. Refrigerate overnight. Stuff into medium 35 mm hog (2") casings. Place cake pan filled with water in bottom of oven. Bake sausage in 170°-190° oven for about 4 hours or until inside temperature is 155°. Spray oven occasionally. Cool sausage down immediately with cold water. Cold smoke if desired.

Venison Sausage Sticks

This recipe calls for equal volumes of pork and venison. Good results are also obtained by using less pork and more venison, up to a ratio of 80% venison and 30% pork.

----

2 # venison	2 1/2 tbsp. dextrose	2 tsp. white pepper
1 # bacon	1/2 tsp. black pepper	1 heaping tbsp. ECA*
3 tbsp. salt	1/2 tsp. garlic powder	cure**
2 tbsp. paprika	5 tbsp. liquid smoke (optional)	

----

*ECA: Encapsulated citric acid – mix with cold meat prior to stuffing. See p. 14
**Volume of cure depends on type of cure used. See p.10

Chill meat thoroughly. Grind meat through 1/4" plate. Add all other ingredients. Mix well. Refrigerate overnight. Stuff into small sheep or collagen casings. Place cake pan filled with water in bottom of oven. Bake at 170° for 2-4 hours or until inside temperature is 155°. Cool sausage down immediately with cold water. Cold smoke if desired. Hang in a cool place for 2-3 days.

Venison Sweet Pickle Loaf

Sliced thin, sweet pickle loaf makes excellent sandwich meat. For a great appetizer, wrap an asparagus tip or green onion in a slice of pickle loaf spread with Mayonnaise.

- -

2 1/2 # venison	4 tbsp. corn syrup
2 1/2 # pork	1/2 tbsp. coriander
2 cups water	2 1/2 tbsp. onion powder
3 1/2 tbsp. salt	1 1/2 tsp. ground celery seed
1 cup nonfat dry milk	1 tsp. white pepper
1/2 cup soy protein powder	cure* (optional)
2 1/2 cups diced sweet pickle	

A high ratio of 70% venison to 30% pork can be use successfully in this recipe.

- -

*Volume of cure depends on type of cure used. See p.10

Grind meat through 1/4" plate several times. Mix all ingredients well and refrigerate overnight. Pack firm into bread pans. Bake at 170° for about 8 hours or until inside temperature is 155°. The mixture can also be stuffed into 3-4" casings, covered with water and simmered on low temperature (180°) until the inside temperatures reaches 150°. Cool immediately.

Venison Olive Loaf

Venison olive loaf is similar to venison pickle loaf for its appeal in a sandwich or as an appetizer. It differs in the unique flavor the olives, mace, and ginger impart. A high ratio of 70% venison to 30% pork can be used successfully in this recipe.

3 1/2 # venison	2 1/2 cups olives with pimentos	1/4 tsp. mace
1 1/2 # pork	1/2 cup soy protein powder	1 tsp. white pepper
3 1/2 tbsp. salt	1 cup nonfat dry milk	5 tbsp. corn syrup
2 cups water	1/2 tsp. ginger	cure* (optional)

*Volume of cure depends on type of cure used. See p.10

Grind meat through 1/4" plate several times. Mix all ingredients well and refrigerate overnight. Pack firm into bread pans. Bake at 170° for about 8 hours or until inside temperature is 155°. The mixture can also be stuffed into 3-4" casings, covered with water and simmered on low temperature (180°) until the inside temperatures reaches 150°. Cool immediately.

Sicilian Pepperoni Sticks

This mild, moist pepperoni stick can be eaten hot or cold. Add liquid smoke for a smoky flavor. For a hotter sausage, add more red pepper flakes.

- -

2 # venison	2 tsp. paprika	1 tsp. anise
2 # pork	1 1/2 tsp. black pepper	1 cup water
1 # bacon or hard fat back	1/4 tsp. ascorbic acid	1 cup red wine
3 tbsp. salt	1 cup nonfat dry milk	2 tbsp. corn syrup solids
4 tsp. ground fennel	2 tsp. dextrose or table sugar	cure*
1 tbsp. red pepper flakes	1/2 cup soy protein powder	

- -

*Volume of cure depends on type of cure used. See p.10

Freeze bacon, chill pork and venison thoroughly. Grind meat through 1/4" plate. Add all other ingredients. Mix well. Refrigerate overnight. Stuff into small 20-25 mm sheep or collagen casings. Place cake pan filled with water in bottom of oven. Bake at 170° for 2-4 hours or until inside temperature is 155°. Cool sausage down immediately with cold water. Cold smoke if desired. Hang in a cool place for 2-3 days.

Andouilli Sticks

Adding water, nonfat dry milk, and soy protein powder to the andouilli recipe (p. 43) produces a moist, tender snack stick. Andouilli sticks also work well as breakfast sausage when steamed and browned quickly.

- -

2 # venison	1/8 tsp. cayenne	1/2 tsp. paprika
2 # pork	1/8 tsp. chili powder	cure*
1 # bacon or hard fat back	1/4 tsp. ground bay leaves	
2 tbsp. salt	1/2 cup soy protein powder	
3 1/2 tbsp. garlic	1/4 tsp. sage	
1/2 tsp. black pepper	1 cup nonfat dry milk	

- -

*Volume of cure depends on type of cure used. See p.10

Freeze bacon, chill pork and venison thoroughly. Grind meat through 1/4" plate. Add all other ingredients. Mix well. Refrigerate overnight. Stuff into small 20-25 mm sheep or collagen casings. Place cake pan filled with water in bottom of oven. Bake at 170° for 2-4 hours or until inside temperature is 155°. Cool sausage down immediately with cold water. Cold smoke if desired. Hang in a cool place for 2-3 days.

Cheddar Cheese Sausage

Imitation cheese should be used here because it has a much higher melting temperature than regular cheese. If regular cheese is used, take care to prevent the cheese from melting during cooking by using low cooking temperatures and cooling quickly.

- -

2 # venison	2 tsp. mustard seed	3 tsp. Accent
2 # pork	1/2 tsp. nutmeg	1 tbsp. paprika
1 # bacon or hard fat back	1/2 tsp. garlic powder	cure*
2 tbsp. salt	2 tbsp. corn syrup solids	
2 tsp. dextrose	1 1/2 cup shredded cheddar cheese	

- -

*Volume of cure depends on type of cure used. See p.10

Keep cheese, pork and venison very cold. Grind meat through 1/4" plate. Add all other ingredients. Mix well. Refrigerate overnight. Stuff into large 35-40 mm (3") casings. Place cake pan filled with water in bottom of oven. Bake at 170° for 4-6 hours or until inside temperature is 155°. Cool sausage down immediately with cold water. Cold smoke if desired.

Venison Romano Sausage

This popular southern Italian sausage should be eaten within several days as the cheese can become quite strong and overwhelm the spices.

- -

1 1/2 # venison	1 cup red wine
1 1/2 # pork	1 tbsp. ground fennel
1 # bacon or hard fat back	1 tsp. garlic powder
1 tbsp. salt	1 tbsp. red pepper flakes
1 tbsp. black pepper	1 cup Romano cheese

- -

*Volume of cure depends on type of cure used. See p.10

Keep cheese, pork, and venison very cold. Chop cheese into 1/4" cubes. Grind meat through 3/8" plate. Add all other ingredients. Mix well. Refrigerate overnight. Stuff into medium 35mm (2") casings. Place cake pan filled with water in bottom of oven. Bake sausage in moist oven until inside temperature is 155°. Cool sausage down immediately with cold water.

Fat Facts

Commercial sausage may contain from 30 to 60 percent fat.
Hard fatback from hogs is the fat of choice for sausage. Beef fact is used in some summer sausage but is too grainy for fresh sausage. Poultry fat melts to quickly at low temperatures. Whitetail fat is too strong flavored. Kidney fat is too hard but may be used in some hard salamis for visual effect. Bacon fat is semi-soft but will work as a substitute for hard fatback if low cooking temperatures are maintained until inside temperature of the sausage reaches 155 degrees. .
--Less fat is need with coarse ground meat--

FINE-TEXTURED SAUSAGE

This chapter contains recipes for both fresh and semi-dried sausages that require different grinding and cooking techniques to produce a fine textured, moist product. Fine-textured fresh sausages include liverwurst, the French gayette and the English faggot. Wieners, mortadella, and bologna are examples of semi-dried sausages that require fine grinding and slow cooking. Grinding the meat through a 1/16-inch plate or chopping small volumes in a food processor achieves the fine texture. If neither option is available, grind the meat several times through a 3/16- or 1/8-inch plate.

Also, slow, moist cooking is the general rule for these recipes. Such cooking prevents a sausage from bursting and the fat from melting while maintaining a moist, smooth texture. Large sausages, like liverwurst and bologna, are actually submerged in 180 degree water or gravy, then the heat is reduced to 160 degrees until the inside temperature of 150 degrees is reached. Here, like in many recipes, it's necessary to have an accurate meat thermometer to register these finished temperatures.

Many older, traditional recipes, like the English faggot or French gayette, recommend using caul (p.4) to enclose the sausage mixture rather than using casings. Some older recipes also call for submerging the sausage in sausage brine for several days followed by smoking and cooking. For sausage brine, combine one gallon of water with one-half cup of canning salt— enough to float an egg—and a pinch of baking soda (1/8 teaspoon or less). Add a quart of dry white wine and heat to boiling. Remove immediately from heat. Add a cloth bag containing a tablespoon of peppercorns, 2 teaspoons of whole cloves and one-half teaspoon of cinnamon. Cool the brine down completely before removing the spices and submerging any sausage. Submersion for a large sausage (40-50mm/3"-4" casing) like mortadella may require 10 days. Medium-cased sausages like bologna (35mm/2") require only two or three days. Smoking usually follows brining followed by cooking in near-boiling water until inside temperature reaches 155 degrees.

Some raw onions have a metallic taste that is eliminated by blanching the onion in water for 60 seconds before adding to a sausage recipe.

Liver Crepinettes

The French term "crepinettes" covers many varieties of small, minced sausages usually made of lamb or pork wrapped in caul (p.4). Traditionally, the sausage is a flattish oval, coated with melted butter or beaten eggs, rolled in breadcrumbs, and grilled.

1/4 # venison liver	1/2 tsp. parsley
1/4 # ham fat or bacon	1/2 tbsp. salt
1/2 # ham	1 tsp. pepper
1 large egg	1/2 cup chopped mushrooms
2 tbsp. thick white sauce	1 cup breadcrumbs

Grind venison and pork through a 1/16" plate or chop small amounts fine with a food processor. If neither option is available, grind meat several times through a 1/8" or 3/16" plate. Beat egg and add 1/2 beaten egg to white sauce. Combine meat, white sauce, mushrooms, parsley, salt, and pepper. Mix well. Wrap in venison or pig caul. Brush with remaining egg, roll in fine breadcrumbs and gently fry in butter or good olive oil.

Venison Faggot

Faggots are a type of English liver sausage with numerous regional variations that traditionally used pig liver as the main ingredient. Adding pig liver to the following recipe gives the sausage a somewhat lighter texture.

---

1 1/2 # venison liver	1/2 cup Saltine cracker crumbs
1 # salt pork	1/4 tsp. black pepper
1/4 cup milk	2 slightly beaten eggs
2 tbsp. salt	1/4 tsp. nutmeg
1 medium onion, chopped	

For a real treat, try a plain faggot patty coated in cracker crumbs then quickly browned in a bit of butter and olive oil.

Soak the cracker crumbs in milk. Cut liver into 1/2" slices then parboil for 3 minutes. Grind onion, liver, and salt pork through a 1/16" plate or chop small amounts fine with a food processor. If neither option is available, grind meat several times through a 1/8" or 3/16" plate. Add cracker crumbs, spices, and eggs to meat mixture. Wrap in pig caul (see p.4) or stuff into 1" collagen or sheep casings. Place in heavy skillet with 2 tablespoons of olive oil and a little water, cover and steam for several minutes, then brown.

Venison Gayettes

The following recipe is a take-off on the French gayette. A basic gayette recipe generally contains pig liver, pork, garlic, salt, and pepper. Variations reflect individual or regional tastes.

----

1 1/2 # venison liver	2 tsp. dried turkey gravy mix
1 # pork or bacon	1 cup herb flavored breadcrumbs
6 tsp. dried onion soup mix	1 tsp. garlic
1/2 cup chicken stock	1 cup liquid beef gravy
1 medium onion, chopped	

Combine chicken stock and breadcrumbs. Cut liver into 1/2" slices then parboil for 3 minutes. Grind onion, bacon, and liver through a 1/16" plate or chop small amounts fine with a food processor. If neither option is available, grind meat several times through a 1/8" or 3/16" plate. Combine all ingredients. Wrap in pig caul (see p.4) or stuff into 1" collagen or sheep casings. To cook, place in baking pan, add beef gravy and bake at 350° for 40 minutes or until brown.

Liverwurst

This is a wonderful liver sausage that's easily sliced. A softer version that will serve as a pate' is achieved by adding 1/2 cup nonfat dry milk to the mix.

1 # venison liver	3/4 tsp. allspice
1 # pork or bacon	1/2 tbsp. dextrose
1/2 # bacon	1/2 tbsp. onion powder
1 1/2 tbsp. salt	2 tbsp. paprika
3/4 tsp. marjoram	Pinch of salt
1 tsp. white pepper	1 tbsp. ground red pepper (optional)

Slice liver into 1/2" slices then parboil for 3 minutes. Grind pork, bacon, and liver through a 1/16" plate or chop small amounts fine with a food processor. If neither option is available, grind meat several times through a 1/8" or 3/16" plate. Combine all ingredients. Stuff into medium-large 35-40mm (3") pig casings. To cook, submerge in salted water heated to 170°. Cover and simmer until inside sausage temperature reaches 155°. Then, cool quickly by spraying with cold water or submerging in ice water.

Venison Bologna

This is an excellent, mild-flavored bologna. The same recipe produces a wiener-type product by simply using smaller casings.

- -

2 # venison	1/2 tbsp. ground coriander
3 # pork	1/2 tbsp. mace
1 cup water	1/2 tbsp. onion powder
3/4 cup Tender Quick®*	1 cup nonfat dry milk
1/2 tbsp. white pepper	1 tbsp. liquid smoke (optional)
1 tbsp. dextrose or table sugar	1 tbsp ground red pepper (optional)

- -

2 1/2 tbsp. of salt and a cure will substitute for Tender Quick®

Grind venison and pork through a 1/16" plate or chop small amounts fine with a food processor. If neither option is available, grind meat several times through a 1/8" or 3/16"plate. Combine all ingredients. Stuff into medium-large 35-40mm (3") casings. To cook, submerge in salted water heated to 170°. Cover and simmer until inside sausage temperature reaches 150°. Then, cool quickly by spraying with cold water or submerging in ice water. A cold smoke is optional but adds a definite flavor and color.

Venison Ring Bologna

Venison ring bologna is a great recipe passed down from generations of Finns who at one time smoked the sausage in their smoke saunas while enjoying a hot, moist sauna. Even today ring bologna hang in some saunas where temperatures of 150 to 200 degrees do a fine job of cooking the delicacy.

- -

1 1/2 # venison	1 tbsp. sugar	1 tbsp. ground celery seed
2 1/2 # pork	1/4 tsp. ginger	1 tsp. coriander
1 # fat pork or bacon	1 tbsp. onion powder	1 3/4 cups venison stock or water
1/4 cup Tender Quick®*	1/2 tbsp. white pepper	1 tbsp. paprika
3/4 cup nonfat dry milk	3/4 tsp. ground cloves	

- -

2 1/2 tbsp. of salt and a cure will substitute for Tender Quick®

Grind venison and pork through 1/16" plate or chop small amounts fine with a food processor. If neither option is available, grind meat several times through a 1/8" or 3/16" plate. Combine all ingredients. Stuff into tender medium 35mm (2") casings. To cook, submerge in salted water heated to 170°. Cover and simmer until inside sausage temperature reaches 150°. Then, cool quickly by spraying with cold water or submerging in ice water. A cold smoke is optional but adds a definite flavor and color.

DRY-CURED SAUSAGE

Basically, dry-cured sausage differs from semi-dry sausage in volume of salt, time spent aging and the *absence* of cooking. Aging can last from one to six months depending on such factors as casing size, relative humidity and temperature, use of accelerators, air circulation, and whether or not smoking is involved. During this time, bacteria and other harmful organisms are killed while the meat marinates and ferments in the spiced oils and water. Whereas, five or six tablespoons of salt may be used for 10 pounds of a semi-dried sausage, nine or 10 tablespoons of salt might be recommended for 10 pounds of a dried salami.

There may also be variations in the type and amount of sugar, liquid, and cure used. As a rule, dextrose sugar is better than table sugar for sausages requiring protracted aging. Fillers and binders such as nonfat dry milk, breadcrumbs, rusk, and soy protein powder are seldom used in dry-cured recipes. The drying process itself provides sufficient body and texture although corn syrup solids seem to bestow a degree of moistue that's worth consideration. Professional sausage makers also recommend a nitrate cure be used in place of a nitrite cure. Mortons® Tender Quick® contains both nitrites and nitrates. Prague Powder #1 and Instacure #1 are used for semi-dry sausage while Prague Powder #2 and Instacure #2 are used for dry-cured sausage (see p.10). Cure accelerators, though not essential, speed the curing process and help retain color. One-half teaspoon of ascorbic acid is sufficient for 10 pounds of meat (see p.12).

Most dry-cured varieties also benefit from a maturation period of one or two days at 70 degrees before extended aging at cooler temperatures. *It should be noted that temperature and moisture control is essential to the production of dry-cured sausage.* Temperatures for aging should range from 45 to 50 degrees with a relative humidity at 70 percent but ranges of 60 to 80 percent work in most cases. Some basements and root cellars are sufficiently cool and humid as are humidifier trays in modern refrigerators. If a refrigerator is used, rest the sausages on small wire racks to insure adequate air circulation. Where necessary, place a small water-filled container in the humidifier to maintain additional moisture. Remove mold that forms on the casings by gently rubbing with a vinegar-soaked sponge. The white, mold-like yeast that forms in four to six weeks is beneficial and need not be removed.

Some old timers recommend "case cleaning" prior to aging, a process that allows for more rapid drying. My family's technique was to submerge a sausage in salted water for one or two hours followed by a one-minute hot water bath. Finally, it's very important to pack casings as tight as possible thereby eliminating air pockets. Air pockets harbor undesirable bacteria resulting in off-colored, offensive products.

Venison Pepperoni

For this recipe, it's best to grind the anise seeds and red pepper flakes rather than use the powdered varieties.

- -

2 # venison	1/2 tsp. allspice
2 # pork	1 1/2 tsp. anise seed
1 # fat pork or bacon	2 1/2 tbsp. paprika
1 1/2 tbsp. ground red pepper	1 tbsp.+1 tsp. corn syrup solids
3 1/2 tbsp. salt	1/4 tsp. ascorbic acid (optional)
5 tsp. dextrose	cure*

- -

*Volume of cure depends on type of cure used. See p. 10

Grind venison and pork through a coarse plate. Mix all ingredients with meat. Stuff into 30-35mm (1 1/2 ") casings. Puncture all air holes and pack tightly. Mature for 1-2 days at 70°. Age in humid place at 40°-50° and about 70% relative humidity approximately 6 weeks.

Wipe any mold that forms with a cloth dipped in vinegar.

Sicilian Venison Pepperoni

This excellent recipe is a variation on the spicy Italian recipe on page 33. The additional salt and cure permits a longer shelf life while the wine and cheese add flavor.

- -

2 # venison	1 tbsp. red pepper flakes
2 # pork	1 1/2 tsp. black pepper
1 # fat pork or bacon	2 tbsp. paprika
1 1/2 tbsp. ground red pepper	1 tbsp. grated Parmesan cheese
4 tbsp. salt	1/2 cup red wine
2 tsp. dextrose	1 tsp. anise seed
2 tbsp. corn syrup solids	cure*

Dried sausage is some-times covered with white yeast that is important and harmless.

- -

*Volume of cure depends on type of cure used. See p. 10

Freeze bacon. Grind venison, and pork through a coarse plate. Grind bacon through a fine plate. Mix all ingredients with meat. Stuff into 30-35mm (1 1/2 ") casings. Puncture all air holes and pack tightly. Mature for 1-2 days at 70°. Age in humid place at 40°-50° and about 70% relative humidity approximately 6 weeks.

Hunters Sausage

This popular sausage has a German origin where it was part of a hunter's or soldier's field rations. Before smoking, the 5"-6" links were pressed into wooden molds giving the sausage its distinct flattened finish.

- -

2 1/2 # venison	1/2 tsp. ground caraway seed
2 1/2 # pork	1 tsp. ground coriander
4 1/2 tbsp. salt	1 tbsp. ECA (see p.14)
2 1/2 tsp. dextrose	1/4 tsp. ascorbic acid (optional) (see p.12)
3 tbsp. corn syrup solids	cure*

- -

*Volume of cure depends on type of cure used. See p. 10

Keep pork very cold. Grind venison and pork through a coarse plate. Mix all ingredients with meat. Stuff into 30-35mm (1 1/2") casings. Puncture all air holes and pack tightly. If sausage is to be flattened in mold, pack loosely. Mature for 1-2 days at 70°. Cold smoke for 4-5 hours. Age in humid place at 40°-50° and about 70% relative humidity approximately 6 weeks.

Endini Salami

A family recipe from northern Italy that remains popular in northern Michigan and Pennsylvania. A wonderful tasting sausage is achieved by boiling this sausage after aging for only 4 weeks.

- -

3 # venison	1/4 tsp. cinnamon	2 cloves crushed garlic
6 # pork	2 tbsp. black pepper	1 tsp. ground nutmeg
1 # fat pork or bacon	3 tbsp. dextrose	1/2 tsp. ascorbic acid (optional) (see p.12)
9 tbsp. salt	1/2 tsp. mace	cure*
1/2 tsp. ground cloves	1/2 cup red wine	
5 tbsp. corn syrup solids	1 tbsp. whole black pepper (optional)	

- -

*Volume of cure depends on type of cure used. See p. 10

Combine wine and garlic. Grind meat through a coarse plate. Combine all ingredients with ground meat and mix well. Stuff into 40mm (3") casings. Puncture all air holes and pack tightly. Mature for 1-2 days at 70°. Age in humid place at 40°-50° and about 70% relative humidity approximately 8 weeks. (Dried in medium 35mm casings results in a great salamini sausage.)

Garlic Salami

Garlic salami is a Genoa-type salami containing garlic and red wine that's usually dried to 70% of its original or green weight.

- -

2 # venison	1/4 cup red wine
2 # pork	1 1/2 tbsp. garlic powder
1 # fat pork or bacon	1 tsp. white pepper
4 1/2 tbsp. salt	1 1/2 tbsp. peppercorns
2 tsp. thyme	1/4 tsp. mace
5 tbsp. corn syrup solids	1/2 tsp. ascorbic acid (optional) (see p.12)
3 tbsp. dextrose	cure*

- -

*Volume of cure depends on type of cure used. See p. 10

Combine wine and garlic. Grind meat and fat through a coarse plate. Combine all ingredients with ground meat and mix well. Stuff into 40mm (3") casings. Puncture all air holes and pack tightly. Mature for 1-2 days at 70°. Age in humid place at 40°-50° and about 70% relative humidity approximately 8 weeks.

Dried Venison Chorizo

Chorizo has numerous regional and individual variations, many of which have been converted to dry-cured recipes. The red pepper with a touch of cumin gives this sausage a pepperoni-like flavor.

- -

1 1/2 # venison	1/3 cup vinegar
2 # pork	2 tsp. red pepper
1/2 # fat pork or bacon	1 tsp dextrose
3 1/2 tbsp. salt	1 tsp.oregano
1 tsp black pepper	1/4 tsp. cumin
1 1/2 tbsp. corn syrup solids	1/2 tsp. ascorbic acid (optional) (see p.12)
	cure*

- -

*Volume of cure depends on type of cure used. See p. 10

Combine wine and garlic. Grind meat and fat through a coarse plate. Combine all ingredients with ground meat and mix well. Stuff into 35-40mm (3") casings. Puncture all air holes and pack tightly. Mature for 1-2 days at 70°. Age in humid place at 40°-50° and about 70% relative humidity approximately 8 weeks.

Juniper Salami

Juniper berries, Fine Herbs—a trade name—and brown sugar give this sausage a marvelous taste with a faint lingering tang. Fine Herbs is a blend of the classic quartet chervil, chives, parsley, and tarragon available at all large food markets.

- -

3 # venison	3 tsp black pepper	cure*
2 # pork	2 tsp. ground juniper berries	
1 # fat pork or bacon	6 tsp. garlic powder	
4 tbsp. salt	1/2 tsp. Fine Herbs	
1 tbsp. brown sugar	1 tbsp. dextrose	
5 tbsp. corn syrup solids	1/2 tsp. ascorbic acid (optional) (see p.12)	

- -

*Volume of cure depends on type of cure used. See p. 10

Combine wine and garlic. Grind meat and fat through a coarse plate. Combine all ingredients with ground meat and mix well. Stuff into 35-40mm (3") casings. Puncture all air holes and pack tightly. Mature for 1-2 days at 70°. Age in humid place at 40°-50° and about 70% relative humidity approximately 8 weeks.

Fennel Salami

This mild, sweet salami has a nice texture and great color with a prevailing hint of garlic and fennel.

- -

2 # venison	1 tsp dextrose	cure*
2 # pork	1 tsp garlic powder	
1 # fat pork or bacon	1 1/2 tsp. crushed anise seed	
3 1/2 tbsp. salt	2 tbsp. crushed fennel seed	
1 tsp black pepper	1/4 cup red wine	
1 1/2 tbsp. corn syrup solids	1/2 tsp. ascorbic acid (optional) (see p.12)	

- -

*Volume of cure depends on type of cure used. See p. 10

Freeze bacon. Combine wine and garlic. Grind meat and bacon through 1/4" plate. Combine all dry spices with ground meat. Add wine. Mix a second time. Stuff into 35-40mm (3") casings. Puncture all air holes and pack tightly. Mature for 1-2 days at 70°. Age in humid place at 40°-50° and about 70% relative humidity approximately 8 weeks.

SUMMER SAUSAGE

Summer sausage is a type of semi-dry sausage (cervelat) that, historically, was made in the early winter but, because of its holding qualities, lasted through spring and summer. There are many varieties of summer sausage. The purpose here is to illustrate several techniques used to create these varieties. All generally contain beef and pork, are seasoned with garlic and then smoked. Their longevity in the past was the result of curing the meat in brine then mixing it with uncured hard back fat and spices before grinding, stuffing, and smoking. The result was a sausage with a semi-dry-texture, color, and feel but with a shelf life much like a dry-cured product. During aging, the combination of bacteria, cured meat, and fat also generated a sour flavor that, over time, became characteristic of summer sausage.

In recent years, summer sausage products are more defined by their sour taste than their long shelf life. While some sausage maker still use brined meat and a long fermentation process to produce the sour flavor, many use fresh meat along with Fermento or encapsulated citric acid (see p.14). Fermento is a dairy product that should be refrigerated until used. It also requires a fermentation period after mixing and before cooking. To ferment, hold the sausage at 90 to 100 degrees with a relative humidity of 70 percent for one or two days. It's easy to duplicate this environment with small volumes of meat by simply letting the sausage rest in a plastic bag, in a warm place for several days. If ECA is used, care must be taken to mix the acid into *cold* meat after grinding and before mixing. No fermentation period is required when using ECA. Some older recipes used vinegar or lemon juice to produce the sour taste.

Summer sausage can be made with pure venison or with varying amounts of pork. Lacking binders, pure venison sausage has a coarse and crumbly texture. Twenty percent pork fat or bacon (one pound pork to four pounds venison) will suffice to produce a nice texture. The addition of 1 cup nonfat dry milk and 1 cup water to a five-pound recipe functions as a binder with no loss of taste. A good process to follow is to coarse grind the meat, add the salt and spice and refrigerate for two days. Next, regrind through a 1/4-inch plate and pack tight into casings.

Morton Tender Quick®

Tender Quick® contains both salt and cure and can be used wherever salt and cure are recommended. A tablespoon of Tender Quick® equal about 1 1/2 tablespoons of salt + cure. The recommended amount of Tender Quick® for 10 pounds of meat is 1/2 cup or 1 1/2 teaspoon per pound.

Old Fashion Summer Sausage

This recipe combines the old technique of using cured meat in the sausage with slow cooking in a modern oven to insure a safe product.

3 # venison	1/4 tsp. coriander	1 1/2 cup salt
1 # pork	1 tsp white pepper	1 gallon water
1 # bacon	1/2 cup red wine	1 tbsp. ECA (see p.14)
1 1/2 tbsp. salt	1/4 tsp. ginger	cure*(optional)
1/4 tsp. cloves		

> When ground, very cold or frozen bacon will form small round balls of fat that enhance the appearance of a sausage.

*Volume of cure depends on type of cure used. See p. 10

Seperate bacon strips and freeze. Make a brine by dissolving 1 1/2 cups of salt and cure in 1 gallon of water. Submerge venison and pork cubes (not the bacon) completely in cure for 3 days at 35-38°. Remove meat from brine and rinse in cold water, dry for several hours. Grind meat and bacon through 1/8" or 1/4" plate. Mix in spices and red wine. Stuff tight into 40-45mm (3") casings. Hang ovenight at room temperature. Cook in moist oven at 180° until inside temperature is 155° or smoke at 180-200° for about 6 hours.

Venison Summer Loaf

This summer sausage recipe has a slight tang that will match any luncheon meat from your favorite deli.

- -

2 1/2 # venison	1/2 tsp. nutmeg
2 1/2 # pork	1/2 tsp. garlic powder
1/4 cup Tender Quick®	2 tbsp.+ 1 tsp. ECA (see p.14)
1 1/2 tbsp. sugar	1/2 tbsp. ground mustard
1/2 tbsp. pepper	Liquid smoke (optional)

- -

*ECA: Encapsulated citric acid – mix to cold meat prior to stuffing

Grind meat through a 1/8" or 1/4" plate. Mix all ingredients with meat. Stuff into 40-45mm (3") casings. Refrigerate ovenight. Place cake pan filled with water in bottom of oven. Bake at 180° for about 5 hours or until inside temperature is 155°. Spray oven occasionally. Spray with cold water to cool sausage down immediately. Cold smoke if desired.

> Try substituting ECA with a tablespoon of white vinegar or lemon juice.

Trenary Summer Sausage

The author used both Fermento and encapsulated citric acid to produce the sour taste so characteristic of summer sausage in this recipe. Encapsulated citric acid produced the best results.

- -

4 # venison	1/2 tsp. ginger
1 # pork	1/2 tsp. mustard seed
1/4 cup Tender Quick®	1/2 tsp. ground mustard
1 1/2 tbsp. sugar	1/2 tsp. garlic powder
1/2 tbsp. coriander	3 tbsp. corn syrup solids
1/2 tsp. pepper	2 tbsp.+ 1 tsp. ECA (see p.14)

- -

*ECA: Encapsulated citric acid – mix to cold meat prior to stuffing

Grind meat through a 1/8" or 1/4" plate. Mix all ingredients with meat. Stuff into 40-45mm (3") casings. Refrigerate ovenight. Place cake pan filled with water in bottom of oven. Bake in 180° oven for about 5 hours or until inside temperature is 155°. Spray oven occasionally. Spray with cold water to cool sausage down immediately. Cold smoke if desired.

Mustard Summer Sausage

Long cold smoking is the key to this recipe. Too much heat will shrink and cook the meat before it is properly smoked. The combination of mustard, coriander, and garlic gives the sausage a distinct flavor. One-cup imitation cheddar or mozzarella (see p.14) improves texture and taste.

- -

3 # ground venison	1 1/2 tbsp. coarse black pepper	1 tsp onion powder
2 # ground pork	2 tbsp. mustard seed	1 tsp. garlic powder
1/4 cup Tender Quick®	2 tsp. coriander seed	
5 tsp. sugar	2 tbsp.+ 1 tsp. ECA (see p.14)	

- -

*ECA: Encapsulated citric acid – mix to cold meat prior to stuffing.

Mix Tender Quick®, venison, pork, and sugar. Place in plastic bag and refrigerate for 2 days. Add remaining ingredients and refrigerator for another 2 days. Stuff into 40-45mm (3") casings. Refrigerate 1 day. Cold smoke for about 8 hours leaving the smoke-house door slighly ajar if necessary. Hot smoke or cook in oven at 200° until inside temperature reaches 150°. Spray with cold water to cool sausage down immediately.

Venison Thuringer

Thuringer is a German invention that benefits from slow fermentation and light smoking. Not a true summer sausage, thuringer can be eaten either fresh or cooked.

- -

4 # venison	5 tsp. dextrose	cure*
1 # pork	1/2 tsp. mustard seed	
3 tbsp. salt	1/2 tsp. coriander	
1 tbsp. pepper	1/2 tsp. celery seed	
1/4 tsp. nutmeg	1/2 tsp mace	
1/2 tsp. ground caraway	2 tbsp.+ 1 tsp. ECA (see p.14)	

- -

*Volume of cure depends on type of cure used. See p. 10

Grind meat through a 1/8" or 1/4" plate. Mix all ingredients with meat. Stuff into 40-45mm (3") casings. Refrigerate ovenight. Place cake pan filled with water in bottom of oven. Bake in 180° oven for about 5 hours or until inside temperature is 155°. Spray oven occasionally. Spray with cold water to cool sausage down immediately. Cold smoke if desired.

Baked Venison Log

Baked Venison Log is popular because it's easy to make and requires no special equipment. Although not a true summer sausage, the baking gives it a firm summer sausage quality. Adding encapsulated citric acid to the mix (see p.14) will add the tang so characteristic of that sausage.

----

5 # ground venison	2 1/2 tsp. garlic salt
1/2 tsp. pepper	2 1/2 tsp. mustard seed
2 1/2 tsp. liquid smoke	3/4 tsp. Tender Quick®

----

*Volume of cure depends on type of cure used. See p. 10

Mix all ingredients with meat. Seal tightly in a plastic bag. Eliminate all air and refrigerate for 3 days. Mix well each day. Moisten hands and roll into sausage-type logs, about 8" long and 2" wide. Bake for 4 hours at 180°. Raise temperature to 300° and bake for 20 minutes.

JERKY - CURES - RUBS

Before the days of refrigeration, smoking and salt curing were used to preserve all types of meat. Rubbing salts directly onto large cuts of meat such as hams and shoulder is called dry curing. Over time, spices and sugars (i.e., honey, molasses, brown sugar) were added during the curing process. Although not necessary, sugar adds flavor, acts as a curing agent, binding agent, and softens the hardness of salt. Just how much sugar or honey depends on individual taste. Some recipes call for twice as much salt as sugar, others for less. Spices, like sugar, are not necessary for curing but add flavor.

Morton Salt produces a Smoke-Flavored Sugar Cure® (see p.10) designed specifically for curing large cuts like hindquarters. The cure contains salt, sugar, and cure so the same product is used as both wet and dry cures. If the meat is to be aged, Morton recommends two tablespoons of cure per pound applied directly to the meat in three stages as a dry cure. If aging is not important, 1 to 1 1/2 tablespoons of cure are recommended.

Large cuts, like hams or venison hindquarter, benefit from a combination of dry and wet cures. The ratio of cure to water in a wet brine is one cup Sugar Cure® to four cups water. (See also STOCK – PICKLES & CANNED VENISON page 173 for additional information on wet cures and pickles.) Deep injection of brine with a meat pump or brining syringe speeds up the curing time by curing meat from the inside while dry cures work on the outside. The time required to complete the cure is reduced by about one-third compared to the dry cure method. This process eliminates the risk of meat near the bone spoiling before dry cure penetrates to that depth. Plus, drying of surface tissue is reduced because the outer layer of tissue spends less time in contact with the salt.

Once cured, the meat should be placed in clean, lukewarm water for about one hour. Soaking dissolves much of the excess cure on the surface, distributes the seasoning more evenly, and makes the meat more receptive to smoke. The Morton *Meat Curing Guide* recommends scrubbing cuts with a stiff bristle brush after curing then drying for about three hours to improve cure penetration and reduce the salty taste.

For meats meant for quick consumption, short cures of one or two hours produce adequate results for small cuts. The following recipe, Venison Loin In Caper Sauce (p.81) is a good example of a quick cure that delivers great flavor. Brining time depends as much on a cook's taste and purpose as it does on the size of a cut.

Venison Loin In Caper Sauce

Though the process is simple, the end result is a definite four-star appetizer or entree. The key is a quick cure and, if possible, a light smoke. Used as an appetizer, the loin should be cut very thin. Be sure the caper sauce is not too hot or it will further cook the venison.

- -

1 # venison loin	1/2 cup olive oil
8 cups water	1 tbsp. capers
3/4 cup salt	1 clove minced garlic
1/4 cup sugar	

Some folks cover the cooked cutlets with sautéed onions in 1/4 cup beef stock combined with 1/2 cup sour cream.

- -

Trim loin of fat and connective tissue. Make a wet cure by dissolving sugar and salt in water. Submerge loin in cure for 4 hours. Remove loin and soak in fresh water for 10 minutes. Bake loin in moist oven until an inside temperature of 130° is reached. Dry loin thoroughly, then cold smoke for one hour or rub loin with liquid smoke before cooking. For appetizer, slice loin very thin. Add garlic and capers to hot olive oil and simmer for one minute. Arrange sliced venison in a circle on a plate, cover with *warm* caper sauce and serve.

Soy & Southwest Jerky

The following recipes are simple but tasty ways of making jerky. Smoking jerky in a medium-hot smoker (170-200°) is the most popular way of drying jerky but the kitchen oven produces good results as well.

- -

Soy Sauce Jerky	Sierra Vista Jerky
2 # venison steak	2 # venison steak
9 tbsp. soy sauce	1/2 cup soy sauce
2 1/2 tbsp. lemon juice	1/3 cup lime juice
1 (14 oz.) can beef bouillon	1 1/2 tsp cayenne powder
	3/4 tsp. salt & 1 tsp. sugar

Brushing liquid smoke onto the meat shortly before cooking gives the meat a smoked flavor.

- -

Slice the venison very thin in both cases. Marinate meat in related ingredients overnight. Place on wire racks and bake at 170° until dry but not brittle, about 2 hours. Soy Sauce Jerky has a mild salt content while the bouillon brings out venison's great flavors. In the Southwest cattle states, lime juice, cayenne pepper, and salt are used to flavor and cure thin slices of meat. Sierra Vista Jerky is a hot rendition of this technique. One teaspoon of cayenne generates a medium-hot jerky.

My Favorite Jerky

An old golfing buddy "Billy K" uses a variety of beef cuts with the following recipe to produce a marvelous sweet jerky. His recommended cuts are the top round of beef or venison.

- -

2-3 # venison	1/2 cup soy sauce
1 cup water	1 tsp. onion powder
1/4 cup salt	1 tsp. garlic powder
1/2 cup red wine	Glaze: 2 oz. honey, 2 oz. brown sugar,
1 tsp. crushed red pepper	2 oz. water
6-8 dashes hot sauce	Liquid smoke (optional)
1/3 cup sugar	

- -

Slice venison very thin. Bring water to a boil. Remove from heat and add all dry ingredients. Mix well. Cool. Add soy sauce, wine, and venison. Marinate overnight. Drain and partially dry meat. Glaze with honey, brown sugar, and water mix. Smoke or bake in oven at 170° for about 3 hours or until meat is firm and chewy but not brittle.

Carne Machaca & Eggs

In the Southwest and Mexico, jerky is often pounded into coarse shreds or small chips called carne machaca (p.88). The machaca is then added to soups, stews or in this case eggs. If jerky is unavailable, use moose brisket or venison neck roasts, simmered until tender, shredded, and browned with onions.

- -

1/2 cup shredded jerky	1/2 chopped red pepper
4 eggs slightly scrambled	1/2 chopped green pepper
1 tbsp. olive oil	1 small tomato
1 small onion	Flour tortillas
1 clove garlic, minced	1/4 cup cheddar cheese (optional)

- -

Use a blender to shred jerky into coarse bits. (Food blenders do a better job than food processors which are slower.) Melt oil in heavy skillet. Add onion, peppers, cheese, and tomato to skillet. Stir in eggs. Continue cooking and stirring until eggs are set. Serve with tortillas.

> Very coarse mortars and pestles made from basalt are used in the Southwest to grind the tough jerky.

Cooked Venison Hams

A combination dry and wet cure is required for large hindquarters (see p.79). A meat pump that injects brine deep is an easy, fast, and modern way of curing large cuts of meat. A large hypodermic syringe works and is less expensive. The following 2 recipes are for 1 small 10 # venison hindquarter.

Morton Salt Technique	Traditional Technique
Wet Cure: combine 1/2 cup Tender Quick® with 2 cups water	Wet Cure: combine 1/2 cup salt, 1/2 cup brown sugar & 2 tbsp. cure with 4 cups water.
Dry Cure: 2 cups Tender Quick® 1/2 cup liquid smoke (optional)	Dry Cure: 1 cup salt & 1/2 cup brown sugar 1/2 cup liquid smoke (optional)

Remove as much silver membrane and tendon from the hindquarter as possible. Inject wet cure into all portions of the hindquarter, especially near the bone. Divide the dry cure in half and rub one cup on the surface of the hindquarter. Place in a clean plastic bag. Set in cool area, about 38° for a week. Remove from bag and soak in lukewarm water for 1 hour. Dry thoroughly. Rub on liquid smoke. Cook in oven at low heat or simmer in covered water until inside is 135°.

Venison Confit

Confit is an old European method of cooking and preserving tough cuts of meat that involves simmering the cured cuts in fat. Once cooked and drained the meat is not greasy and makes great warm or cold dishes.

2 venison shanks	1 tbsp. crushed juniper berries
1 bay leaf	1 clove garlic, minced
1/4 tsp. salt	Cure
1 1/2 cups canning salt	Oil to cover shanks
1/4 tsp. cloves	

Mix all dry ingredients. Trim all fat and sinew. Rub dry cure into shanks then place in plastic bag or ceramic bowl and refrigerate for 24 hours. Brush the dry cure from the meat. Place in heavy pot, cover completely with oil. Bring to simmer then reduce heat to low and hold temperature at 200°. Cook slowly at this temperature until meat is tender and easily removed from the bone. Remove from heat, drain, cover, and cool. To preserve indefinitely the old-fashion way, cover with fat and keep cool.

Jerked Venison Ribs

In culinary circles, the word "jerk" refers to Jamaican jerk or jerk rub, a highly pungent, flavorful, seasoned paste used to pack around meats while being smoked, grilled, or braised.

- -

2 1/2 # rack of venison	2 tbsp. cumin seed
2 tbsp. olive oil	2 tbsp. coriander seed
1/4 cup coarse salt	1 tbsp. whole black peppercorn
4 cloves garlic	1 tbsp. allspice berries
4 shallots or 2 medium onions	4 tbsp. brown sugar

- -

In a food processor or blender, pulse seeds, berries, and peppercorns until coarsely ground. Add shallots, garlic, salt, and sugar. Process to a thick paste. Set aside. Rinse venison, pat dry, then rub a thick layer of paste over all the meat. Place in plastic bag and chill for 4 hours or overnight. Rub off excess paste. Heat oil in heavy skillet over medium-high heat. Sear meat on all sides until browned. Place, uncovered, in 450° oven for 15–18 minutes or until meat thermometer reads medium rare, about 135°. Let rest for 5 minutes and slice.

Shredded Venison

Shredded meat is fibrous. Any jerky or cooked venison can be shredded. Jerky is best shredded by pulsing small pieces in a blender. Fried or braised cuts should be cooked until the meat falls from the bones. Fork shredding gives the best results with cooked meat.

Shred into thin, short fibers by holding a slab down with one fork while clawing at it with a second fork. You don't want chunk or powdered venison. You want venison shredded into fibers 1/2" long at the most.

Venison Brisket & Flank

In contrast to the soft-textured neck or shoulder meat, flank and brisket from large game animals like elk, moose, and caribou are dense enough that they require special treatment. Marinating in acidic liquids, like wine, buttermilk, or a vinegar pickle along with slow roasting and thin slicing is recommended for these cuts. Mexican and Southwest chefs use the densest cuts in their crispy, fried tacos, their fried chiviuchangas, in burritos, as well as their bean frijoles.

SLOW ROASTING VENISON

Whereas certain cuts of venison lend themselves to quick cooking, others are best cooked slowly. Slow, moist roasting, called braising or pot-roasting, is the preferred technique for roasts from the hindquarters, shoulders, ribs, and shanks. The humid, low-heat environment tenderizes large tough cuts of meat. The success of braising depends on the small amount of liquid used and slow cooking. It helps to braise in a heavy metal pot with a tight lid to prevent burning and moisture loss.

Low baking temperatures of 275 to 330 degrees are recommended for these cuts. Cooking time depends on size and thickness. A good rule to follow is to cook the meat until it falls from the bone or is easy to cut with a fork. A moist environment means adding more water or stock to the roasting pan during the cooking process. (See p.179 for details on making venison stock.)

Slow roasting whitetail ribs works especially well by melting the tallow that's layered around the bones. Venison tallow around the ribs, back, and flank of whitetail has a distinct taste and texture that is disagreeable to most people and should be replaced with pork fat where necessary. Unlike whitetail, the fat along the large ribs of moose, elk, and caribou is agreeable with little or no aftertaste.

Marinating with vinegar, wine, lemon juice, yogurt, or buttermilk helps tenderize and improve the flavor of some cuts. Allow 1/2-cup marinade for every pound of venison. Soak small pieces of cubed meat for two to three hours, soak a large five-pound cut overnight. Remember, careless cooking robs venison of its unique qualities.

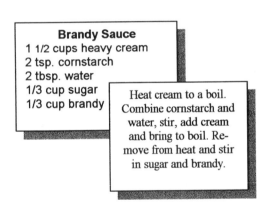

Brandy Sauce
1 1/2 cups heavy cream
2 tsp. cornstarch
2 tbsp. water
1/3 cup sugar
1/3 cup brandy

Heat cream to a boil. Combine cornstarch and water, stir, add cream and bring to boil. Remove from heat and stir in sugar and brandy.

Hunters' Sauce

2 tbsp. butter	16 oz. beef broth
2 tbsp. flour	Salt & pepper
3 tomatoes	1 tbsp. lemon juice
2 onions	1/4 tsp. vinegar
12 small mushrooms	Pinch of thyme, parsley, and bay leaf

Combine flour and butter in heavy skillet. Stir until brown. Add beef broth slowly, stirring to eliminate lumps. Add spices, tomatoes, onions, and mushrooms. Stir in vinegar and lemon juice before serving.

Venison Swiss Steak

Venison Swiss steak, like venison stroganoff, is a traditional dish at many venison cookouts that occur during and after deer season throughout the States.

- -

2 # venison steak	1 clove chopped garlic
1/2 cup flour	3/4 cup chopped onion
1 tsp. salt	1/4 cup chopped celery
3/4 tsp. pepper	1/4 cup chopped green pepper
1/4 cup bacon drippings	1 can chopped tomatoes

- -

Mix salt and pepper to flour. Flour steaks with seasoned flour. Pound both sides of steaks with a mallet adding as much flour as meat will hold. Heat bacon drippings in heavy casserole over medium-high heat. Sear steaks on all sides. Lower heat and add the garlic, onion, celery, pepper, and tomatoes. Cover casserole and bake at 300° for 2 1/2 hours.

Northern Michigan Swiss Steak

Northern Michigan Swiss Steak is a regional version of Swiss steak and is
served with steaks smothered in a thick, brown, onion and mushroom gravy.

- -

2 # venison steak	1 clove chopped garlic
1/2 cup flour	1 cup sliced onion
1 tsp. salt	1/4 cup chopped celery
3/4 tsp. pepper	1/4 cup chopped green pepper
1/4 cup bacon drippings	1 cup venison or beef stock (see p.179)
1 can mushrooms	

- -

Mix salt and pepper to flour. Flour steaks with seasoned flour. Pound both sides of steaks with
a mallet adding as much flour as meat will hold. Heat bacon drippings in heavy casserole over
medium-high heat. Sear steaks on all sides. Remove steak. Add sliced onions and simmer until
onions are caramelized. Lower heat and add the meat, garlic, celery, pepper, mushrooms, and
stock. Cover casserole and bake at 300° for 2 1/2 hours. Remove meat. Make gravy from
drippings and serve with mashed potatoes, mashed rutabagas, and fresh bread.

Venison With Beet Salad

This recipe comes from a Finnish friend who claims beet salad is traditionally served with venison for lunch or dinner along side a baked potato and a glass of buttermilk.

1/2 # venison loin	2 tbsp. sliced green onions
2 tbsp. olive oil	1 tbsp. parsley
Salt and pepper to taste	4 tbsp. Italian dressing
1 cup sliced beets	2 large lettuce leaves
1/2 cup green peas	1 hard boiled egg, chopped

Preheat oven to 450°. Sear venison on all sides in hot oil. Salt and pepper loin. Bake in oven until rare or medium-rare—about 6 minutes or meat thermometer registers 135°. Slice, set aside and keep warm. Combine beets, peas, onions, parsley, and 2 tablespoons of Italian dressing. Top lettuce leaf with 1/2 cup vegetable mix. Add 1 tablespoon of chopped eggs. Set sliced venison next to salad. Drizzle venison with Italian dressing. Repeat with second leaf of lettuce.

Braised Short Ribs of Moose

Unlike whitetail deer with their disagreeable tallow, moose, elk, and caribou have large ribs that are easy to cook with no disagreeable aftertaste.

- -

8 short ribs of moose	6 cloves garlic
Salt and pepper	1 medium onion
3 tbsp. olive oil	2 cups chicken broth
2 carrots	3/4 cup red wine
2 stalks celery	2 cups venison or beef broth (see p.179)

- -

Season ribs with salt and pepper. In heavy roaster, sear ribs on all sides in 3 tablespoons olive oil. Section carrots and celery into large pieces. Slice onion into wedges. Add garlic and vegetables to pan and brown. Add red wine and reduce two-thirds. Add beef and chicken stock and simmer for about 2 hours or until ribs are very tender. Remove vegetables and ribs. Thicken pan liquids with 1 tablespoon of cornstarch that's been dissolved in cold water. Drizzle gravy over ribs and vegetables. Include mashed potatoes or pasta.

Venison Loin With Currant Sauce

Currant jelly is a common ingredient in many European wild game recipes, especially those found in France.

1 venison loin, 6" long
1 tsp. water
1 1/2 tsp. dry mustard
1/4 cup currant jelly
1 1/2 cup brown beef gravy

2 cloves minced garlic
1 tsp. salt
1 tsp. cracked black pepper
1 tsp. rosemary leaves

Dissolve dry mustard in water. Add gravy and currant jelly. Cook over medium heat 5 minutes or until bubbly, stirring occasionally. Set aside. Heat oven to 450°. Combine garlic, salt, pepper, rosemary, and press evenly onto loin. Roast meat about 5 to 7 minutes or until medium-rare (135°) on the meat thermometer. Carve roast into slices. Serve with currant sauce.

Choice cuts such as venison loin with get tough if cooked beyond rare or medium-rare.

Venison Shoulder With Caper Sauce

Venison shoulder is an excellent choice for roasting, especially with whitetail where only small pieces are obtained by boning.

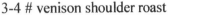

3-4 # venison shoulder roast	3/4 tbsp. lemon juice
2 cups water or white wine	2 tbsp. flour
3 bay leaves	2 tbsp. olive oil
1 medium onion, diced	2 cups venison or beef stock (see p.179)
1/2 cup celery tops	1 tsp. orange juice
1/4 cup parsley	3 tbsp. capers
Salt & pepper	1 cup milk

Place roast in roasting pan. Add water, bay leaves, onion, parsley, celery, lemon juice, salt, and pepper. Bake for 3 hours at 325°. In separate pan, heat olive oil and stir in flour. Add stock slowly, stirring constantly until sauce thickens. Add milk, orange juice, and capers. Simmer for 2 minutes. Slice venison and serve with hot caper sauce.

> For vegetable pot roast, add cubed potatoes and carrots during the last hour of roasting.

Bootleggers Venison

A family recipe that goes back to a time when brandy was made from left-over grape skins, stems, and seeds—the *vinaccia* of wine grapes. Sweetened grappa helps balance the peppery sauce.

- -

1 venison loin, 7" long	1 tsp. butter
Salt and pepper	1 tbsp. flour
2 tbsp. olive oil	1/4 tsp. dried thyme
1 cup chopped onion	1 cup baby peas
1 cup venison or beef stock (see p.179)	1/3 cup whipping cream
2 tsp. ground peppercorns	1/3 cup grappa or brandy

- -

Preheat oven to 425°. Season loin with salt and pepper. Heat oil in heavy skillet over medium-high heat. Brown loin in hot oil on all sides about 2-3 minutes. Transfer to oven and bake until meat thermometer registers 135°. Sauté chopped onion in skillet until translucent, add stock and grappa. Simmer to 1/2 cup. Mix butter and flour to a paste, stir into sauce. Reduce heat. Stir in whipping cream, baby peas, and crushed peppercorns. Simmer until thick. Salt and pepper to taste. Spoon over sliced loin. Serve with roasted sweet potatoes.

Venison Roast in Red Wine

Another family recipe that's guaranteed to stimulate the palate and neutralize any off-odors such as freezer burn. Serve with polenta, rice, or mashed potatoes.

- -

2 # venison roast
2 cloves minced garlic
1 medium sliced onion
5 whole cloves
1/4 tsp. allspice
2 crushed bay leaves

2 cups dry red wine
1/4 cup cubed salt pork
2 tsp. flour
1/2 cup butter
1 cup whipping cream

- -

Combine the roast, garlic, onion, cloves, allspice, bay leaves, and red wine in a plastic or ceramic bowl. Marinate for 1-2 hours. Brown salt pork in a roasting pan. Add 1/2 cup butter, the roast, and one half the marinate. Roast at 300° for 2 1/2 hours adding marinade as needed to keep moist. Remove meat when done. Let rest for 10 mintues then slice and keep warm. Strain pan juice, stir in whipping cream and 2 teaspoons of flour. Cook for 2 minutes. Pour over venison.

Rolled Italian Venison

This is a classic Italian beef braciola that works well with venison. The venison round is butterflied, spread with a mixture of Parmesan cheese, breadcrumbs, and garlic, then rolled and tied.

---

1 # boneless top round	2 tbsp. Parmesan cheese	1 # cooked spagetti
4 strips crumbled bacon	1 clove minced garlic	2 cups spagetti sauce
4 strips uncooked bacon	Parmesan cheese	
Salt and pepper	2 tsp. basil	
1/2 cup breadcrumbs	1/4 cup chopped parsley	

Heat oven to 400°. Carefully butterfly roast into a 3/4" slab then pound to 1/2". Combine crumbled bacon, salt, pepper, breadcrumbs, parsley, 2 tablespoons Parmesan cheese, and garlic. Spread mixture over meat, leaving 1" at narrow ends. Roll in jelly-roll fashion and tie with string at 2" intervals. Cover with remaining bacon strips and roast for 20-25 minutes or until inside temperature is 135°. Let rest for 10 minutes, then slice thinly. Arrange spagetti and venison on platter, cover with spagetti sauce and garnish with parsley, cheese, and basil.

Deviled Venison

Deviled venison is a more healthy, spicy version of Paneed Venison (see p. 109). Those familiar with deviled eggs will recognize the flavor. Scalloped potatoes, makes a great side dish for this recipe.

- -

6 venison steaks, 1/2" thick	1 tsp. grated onion
Salt and cayenne pepper	1 tsp. chopped parsley
1 tbsp. butter	1 clove minced garlic
1 tbsp. liquid mustard	1 tsp. horseradish
1 tbsp. mint jelly	Pinch of nutmeg
1 tbsp. wine vinegar	1 cup Saltine cracker crumbs
1/2 tsp. Worcestershire sauce	3 tbsp. paprika

- -

Season steaks with salt and cayenne, then brush with softened butter. Combine mustard, jelly, vinegar, Worcestershire sauce, onion, parsley, garlic, horseradish, and nutmeg. Spread mixture on both sides of steaks. Dip venison in fine cracker crumbs. Let set for 15 minutes. Arrange steaks on a buttered cookie sheet. Bake in 425° oven for 7 minutes or until brown, turn and brown the opposite side for 7 minutes. Dust with paprika and serve with mint jelly.

Braised Venison Shank

Braised venison shanks are truly delightful. Once tried you will never discard or grind shank scraps for burger again. Following are two simple recipes for cooking this much-maligned cut.

- -

2 large venison shanks
Oil to cover
Salt and pepper to taste

============

Place shanks in roaster and cover with oil. Bake for 2 1/2 hours at 280° or until meat falls from bone. Remove and drain meat immediately. Salt and pepper to taste.

2 large venison shanks
2 cups water
1 bay leaf
10 juniper berries
1/4 tsp. rosemary
1 chopped onion

==========

Place all ingredients in covered roaster and bake for 2 1/2 hours at 320° or until meat falls from the bone.

- -

Both recipes produce excellent results, almost as good as veal shanks. Serve with mint jelly. See also Venison Confit, page 86 for an old European method of cooking venison shanks.

Venison Rolati

Rolatis are miniature triangles of venison, stuffed and rolled. They should be smothered in gravy if served as an entrée. They also make wonderful appetizers. Any good stuffing recipe can be used.

- -

2 # venison steak, 1/2" thick	1/2 cup ham or salami
Salt and pepper	1 clove minced garlic
1 medium onion	2 tbsp. olive oil
2 stalks celery	2 tbsp. buter
1/2 cup mushrooms	Brown sauce or tomato sauce
1/2 green pepper	Tooth picks

- -

Pound venison steaks to 1/4" thick. Cut steaks into triangles, 3" on the side. Chop onion, celery, mushrooms, green pepper, and ham very fine; add garlic and mix well. Place a teaspoon of mixture in center of each triangle. Roll each triangle around mixture and fasten with tooth pick. Heat olive oil and butter to hot but not smoking. Brown meat quickly. Simmer in brown gravy or tomato sauce for 45 mintues. Serve over noodles.

Venison Birds

Thin strips of venison loin, wrapped around small morsels of cheese, pâté and ham, then skewered and braised are often referred to as Venison Birds. Serve on bed of lettuce.

- -

6 venison cutlets from backstrap
Salt & pepper
1/4 # mozzarella
1/4 # thin sliced prosciutto
1/4 # chicken-liver pâté

6 bay leaves
2 (6") skewers
2 tbsp. olive oil
2 tbsp. butter
1/2 cup red wine
1/2 cup venison or beef broth (see p.179)

- -

Flatten cutlets to 3" wide and 5" long. Season with salt and pepper. In blender, combine liver and 3 slices of prosciutto. Blend well. Cut mozzarella into small cubes. Place about 3 rounded teaspoons of liver stuffing and a few mozzarella cubes in center of each cutlet, roll. On each skewer place 3 birds separated by a slice of remaining prosciutto and 1 bay leaf. Brown birds evenly in oil and butter for 5 minutes. Remove from skillet. Add wine and stir until reduced to half, then add broth and simmer for 10 minutes. Add birds, heat, and serve.

Tenderloin in Puff Pastry

This is a simple, yet elegant recipe that does service to the delicate texture and flavor of whitetail tenderloin (see venison tenderloin p.5). The key here is with the puff pastry: A 1/2" ribbon around the edge of each plate will puff and firm nicely. Serve with a light soup and a vegetable.

---

1 1/2 pounds whitetail tenderloin, cubed
1 tbsp. olive oil & 1 tbsp. butter
1/2 # mushrooms
1 cup whole small onions
1 tbsp. tomato paste

1/2 cup white wine
Salt, pepper & 1 clove minced garlic
5 tbsp. butter
1/2 cup water & 1/2 cup flour
2 eggs

Preheat oven to 400°. Sauté venison quickly in hot oil and butter. Add to center of a pie plate. Add mushrooms, onions, tomato paste, garlic, wine, salt, and pepper to pan drippings. Simmer for 2 minutes—or until thickened—over medium-high heat. Pour over venison. Bring butter and water to boil. When butter melts, add flour all at once. Beat vigorously until mix forms a ball. Add eggs one at a time, beating vigorously after each egg. Line the edge of each pie plate with 1/2" ribbon of dough. Bake for 15 minutes or until dough is crispy brown. Serve immediately.

Braised Venison Tongue

Moose, caribou, or elk tongue are most easy to work with simply because of their size. Four whitetail tongues weigh about 2-3 pounds. Tongue should be parboiled and skinned (see p.160) for this recipe.

- -

2-3 # venison tongue	2 tbsp. butter	1 bay leaf
1/2 # lean bacon	1 medium carrot	1/2 cup venison stock (p. 179)
Salt & pepper	1 clove garlic, minced	1/2 cup sherry
1 medium onion	1/4 tsp. thyme	Boiled potatoes
2 leaks	1/2 tsp. parsley	
4 tbsp. flour	1/2 cup red wine	

- -

Roughly chop the onion, leaks, and carrot. Fry the bacon slowly in 2 tablespoons of butter until transparent then add to vegetables. Continue to simmer until onions are transparent. Add garlic, thyme, and parsley until bacon and vegetables are lightly browned. Add flour and stir until brown. Gradually add wine, stock, and bay leaf. Add tongue and cook at low temperature for 2-3 hours. Remove tongue. Reduce stock and flavor with sherry. Pour over sliced tongue and potatoes.

Brandied Apricot Venison

Brandied venison is popular in northern Michigan where rutabagas are standard camp fare. The apricots provides a bit of sweetness that works well with both the venison and rutabaga.

- -

1 # venison steak	2 cups red wine
8 whole cloves	8 oz. dried apricots
8 black peppercorns	1/4 cup vinegar
12 whole allspice	1/4 tsp. cinnamon
1 large onion, sliced thin	1/2 # thin sliced rutabaga
2 tbsp. brandy	1/4 cup parsley

- -

Marinade steak with cloves, peppercorns, allspice, onion, brandy, and 1 cup wine at room temperature for 2-3 hours. Bring to boil vinegar, apricots, cinnamon, 1 cup red wine, and 1 cup water, then simmer for 20 minutes. Drain fruit and set aside. Reduce vinegar sauce by half. Add rutabaga and simmer until firm but fork will pierce easily. Set aside. Remove steak from marinade and roast for 15 minutes, let rest for 5 minutes, then cut into thin slices. Toss venison, apricots, and rutabaga with reduced vinegar sauce. Garnish with parsley.

FRYING – BROILING - GRILLING VENISON

Frying, broiling and grilling are virtually interchangeable since all three are quick methods of cooking venison. Frying, grilling, or broiling venison are usually done with tender cuts including small tenderloins, tender steaks, and cutlets from the backstrap. Since these cuts contain very little fat, it's necessary to cook them quickly, which means medium-high or high temperatures under the broiler, on a grill, or in a heavy skillet with hot oil.

The heavy skillet provides a steady, constant temperature as the meat browns. The hot oil sears the surface and helps seal in moisture. Some folks like half oil and half butter. Regardless, one or two tablespoons of oil are sufficient to sauté several steaks whereas three-fourths cup or more give a deep-fry result. As a rule, use hot—but not smoking—oil for searing and frying.

Broiling and grilling venison can be disheartening if not done correctly. To insure success on the grill and under the broiler it's important to follow some basic rules. First, use a meat thermometer. Follow the recipe's recommended temperature but check the thermometer once or twice especially toward the end as temperatures can rise quickly. Except for whitetail ribs, cook the meat to rare (130-135°), or medium-rare (135-140°), then let the meat rest. Resting allows meat juices to set before slicing.

Second, broil or grill thin steaks—1 inch or less—quickly and at high temperatures. For cuts such as thick steaks, large tenderloins, or whole backstrap, it's helpful to first sear the outside in hot oil at high temperatures before further cooking. Avoid thick cuts over an inch and a half. When grilling, grease the grill with bacon or oil before setting meat. Lower the grill to one inch above the flames to sear, then raise the grill a bit to finish cooking.

Finally, keep the meat moist. Don't be afraid to use acid marinades, like wine and vinegar. They not only keep the meat moist but help tenderize while adding subtle flavors and aromas. If a portion is large or sauce scarce, baste meat with vinegar water to keep it moist until ready for the sauce. Vinegar water is made with one part vinegar to nine parts water. Sauce is best applied just before serving.

Because whitetail ribs contain so much undesirable tallow, they require special handling. For ease of handling, and to expose more tallow, it's best to cut the ribs in half, crosswise, forming two long strips. Next, trim as much tallow as possible and then braise before browning on the grill or under the broiler. Braising—baking the ribs at low temperature in a moist environment—serves to tenderize the meat and melt the tallow. It helps to drain the pan several times during braising. After draining, add additional liquids and finish cooking. In all cases, serve whitetail ribs very hot.

Paneed Venison

"Pane" comes from the French verb "paner" meaning to coat with breadcrumbs. Paneed venison is one of the most popular ways of preparing venison cutlet and steak. Popular additions to this recipe call for a touch of lemon zest, 1 1/2 teaspoon of grated Parmesan cheese, and 1/4 teaspoon of thyme mixed in with the crumbs. The key with panned venison is to fry quickly in hot oil/butter to a crisp brown on both sides.

- -

6 cutlets, 1" thick	1 cup Saltine cracker crumbs
Salt and pepper	3 tbsp. olive & butter
1/2 cup flour	2 beaten eggs in 1/2 cup milk

- -

Pound the cutlets to 1/2" thick. Pat venison dry and season with salt and pepper. Dredge in flour, shaking off the excess. Dip in beaten egg/milk mixture then smother with crackercrumbs. Transfer cutlets to a wire rack and let set for at least 15 minutes and up to 30 minutes. When ready to fry, heat oil and butter until hot but not smoking and quick-fry the cutlets for about 2 minutes or until golden, crisp brown on each side.

Paneed Venison in Hunter Sauce

This is a variation on a classic French recipe for veal cutlets. It follows the recipe for frying cutlets from the previous recipe.

- -

6 cutlets, 1" thick	6 sliced mushrooms
Salt and pepper	1/2 small onion, chopped
1/2 cup flour	2 tbsp. butter
2 beaten eggs in 1/2 cup milk	1/2 cup white wine
1 cup Saltine cracker crumbs	1 cup tomatoes
3 tbsp. olive oil	1/4 cup chopped parsley
3 tbsp. butter	Pinch of tarragon

- -

Prepare cutlets as described in previous recipe with crumbs, milk, eggs and flour. Also, fry in butter and oil as described. Keep the venison warm. Sauté the sliced mushrooms and onion in 1 tablespoon of butter. Add the wine and simmer until reduced by half. Add the tomatoes and again cook until reduced by half. Season with salt. Swirl in last tablespoon of butter until just melted. Finish with chopped parsley and tarragon. Pour over the meat.

Venison Rib Rack

Early planning when butchering is needed here. The process involves cutting the loin in half alone the chine (backbone) and leaving 3" of rib cleaned down from the eye of the loin. Double the recipe for larger rib racks from moose, elk, and caribou.

---

2 # venion rib rack	1/2 cup brown sugar
1/3 cup water	1 (12 oz.) bottle chili sauce
1 tbsp. dry mustard	1 (14 oz.) bottle ketchup

Lightly score the silver membrane along the back of the rack in a diamond pattern. French the bone by removing all fat and meat from the ribs to within 1/2" of the eye. Combine the water, mustard, ketchup, sugar, and chili sauce. Heat to a boil, stirring occasionally, then cool. Place loin in a container, cover with half the sauce and marinate for at least 3 hours, or overnight. Grill or broil over very hot flames until medium-rare. Remove from heat, cover with remaining hot sauce, and serve.

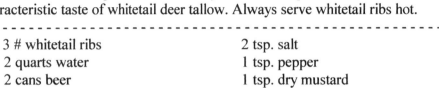

Whitetail Ribs with Honey

The combination of spices, lemon, honey, and beer helps eliminate the
characteristic taste of whitetail deer tallow. Always serve whitetail ribs hot.

- -

3 # whitetail ribs	2 tsp. salt
2 quarts water	1 tsp. pepper
2 cans beer	1 tsp. dry mustard
1 cup honey	2 tsp. ground ginger
2 tbsp. lemon juice	1/2 tsp. ground mustard

- -

Trim ribs of as much fat as possible. Boil ribs for an hour in water and 1 can beer. Make a
marinade of 1 can beer, honey, lemon juice, salt, pepper, mustard, ginger, and nutmeg. Remove
ribs from water and place in marinade for 5-6 hours. Grill over hot coals until brown and crisp.
Baste often with half the sauce. When done, pour remaining sauce over ribs and serve hot.

Frenched Moose/Elk/Caribou Ribs

Compared to whitetail, moose, elk, and caribou provide much larger rib racks with little or no tallow. The following techinque of trimming the bone and fanning the rack affords easy handling and a nice presentations.

- -

2 # ribs, 6" long	1 package dry onion soup mix
3 tbsp. olive oil	1 clove minced garlic
3 tbsp. butter	1 medium onion, sliced
Salt and pepper	1 cup barbecue sauce
1 1/2 cup water or white wine	

- -

Heat oven to 300°. French the ribs by trimming and cleaning—to the bare bone—2" of meat from each rib. The ribs should now have 4" of meat on and between the bone with 2" of bare bone above. From the top, make a 2" cut between each rib so that the ribs are only connected by 2" of meat at the bottom. Salt and pepper ribs. Sear in 3 tablespoons of butter and oil on all sides. Place ribs, soup mix, garlic, sliced onion, and wine in pan, cover and bake 2 hours or until meat is ready to fall from bone. Remove ribs, cover with barbecue sauce and grill or broil for several minutes.

Venison Cutlets With Blue Cheese

Several medium-sized turnips—hollowed and filled with peas and baked in a little butter at 350° until brown—serve as an excellent side dish to these savory cutlets.

- -

4 venison cutlets, 1" thick	1/2 cup brandy
2 tbsp. olive oil	1/4 cup water
Salt and pepper	1/2 tsp. dried rosemary
1/2 cup venison or beef stock (see p.179)	1 cup crumbled blue cheese

- -

Heat olive oil in heavy skillet over medium-high heat. Season cutlets with salt and pepper. Sauté cutlets to rare or medium-rare, about 2 minutes per side. Transfer cutlets to platter, cover, keep warm. Add stock, water, brandy, and rosemary to skillet. Stir in brown bits from pan bottom. Bring to boil and reduce to 3/4 cup. Spoon sauce over cutlets. Top each with 1/4 cup blue cheese.

Paprika Schnitzel Venison

This is an *exceptional* recipe. It's traditionally served with applesauce and/or creamed spinach and potato dumplings. The author will vouch for side dishes of green beans, black morels, and gnocchi. The creamy, onion-filled béchamel sauce and cutlet is a winning combination.

- -

1 1/2 # venison loin	3 medium onions, sliced
1/2 cup flour	1 cup venison or beef stock (see p.179)
Salt & pepper	1/2 cup sour cream
2 tbsp. olive oil	1/2 cup parsley, capers, or anchovies
1 tbsp. paprika	

- -

Slice venison loin into 1/2" thick cutlets. Coat each cutlet with a mixture of flour, salt, and pepper. Heat oil in heavy skillet, add paprika, then sauté onions until transparent. Remove and reserve onions. Sauté meat on both sides to medium-rare. Remove from pan. Add stock and onions to pan. Cover and simmer over low heat for 15 minutes. Add sour cream and season to taste. Smother cutlets with onion mix. Garnish with parsley and capers or anchovies.

Venison Nut Chops

Venison cutlets are similar to lamb chops in that they come from the loin and lend themselves to quick cooking. Venison tenderloin also works well here.

- -

4 venison cutlets, 1" thick   2 eggs
1/3 cup almond crumbs   1 cup flour
1/3 cup pistachio crumbs   2 tbsp. butter
1/3 cup walnut crumbs   2 tbsp. olive oil
1 cup Saltine crackers   Salt and pepper
1/2 cup milk

- -

Combine nut crumbs and cracker crumbs. Whisk eggs and milk together. Coat venison chops with flour, dip in egg/milk mixture, then coat with crumbs. Let set for 15 mintues. Heat olive oil and butter in heavy skillet over medium-high heat. When oil is very hot but not smoking, add cutlets and sauté until golden brown on both sides. Salt and pepper to taste.

For a light cherry sauce, deglaze the skillet with 1 cup white wine, add 1/2 cup dried cherries and reduce to half. Thicken with 1/2 tbsp. cornstarch dissolved in cold water

Venison Cutlet In A Cup

This is an elegant dish that looks time consuming but the microwave helps reduce preparation time to 15-20 minutes. The cups make an excellent side dish to
a salad.

4 cutlet, 1" thick	1 clove minced garlic
2-3 sheets filo dough	2 tbsp. tomato paste
4 tbsp. butter	Salt & pepper
1/2 # frozen spinach	Cup-cake pan
3 tbsp. olive oil	

Heat oven to 400°. Melt butter. Make 4 filo cups by cutting dough into 5" squares. Use 4 squares
per cup. For each cup, brush the 4 squares with melted butter. Lay one on top the other slightly
offsetting the corners. Invert cup-cake pan. Press 4 sheets of filo over cup-cake form and mold
into a cup. Repeat for 3 more cups. Bake until golden brown. Set aside. Drain spinach well and
chop fine. Brown garlic in oil, add tomato paste, and spinach. Cook 15 minutes. Season with salt
and pepper. Microwave each cutlet for 3 minutes. Cutlet should be medium-rare. Place in filo
basket, surround with spinach. Serve warm.

Grilled Venison Backstrap

In marinating and grilling a venison loin, take care to keep the tender, juicy qualities of this choice cut intact. Use a meat thermometer to achieve rare or medium-rare.

- -

2 # venison loin	1/2 tsp. salt
3/4 cup dry red wine	1/2 tsp. ground cardamon seed
2 tbsp. pepper	4 cloves minced garlic
2 tbsp. rosemary	1/2 tsp. anise
2 tbsp. thyme	2 tbsp. red wine vinegar
1 ground bay leaf	3 tbsp. olive oil
1/2 tsp. ground juniper berry	2 tbsp. Dijon mustard
1 tsp. ground coriander	

- -

Combine wine, spices, vinegar, oil, and mustard in plastic bag. Add loin and marinate in refrigerator for 24 hours. Remove venison and broil on very hot grill or under broiler for approximately 4 minutes per side or until medium-rare.

Boilermaker Kabobs

The classic one-two drink called a boilermaker—shot of whiskey with a beer chaser—comes together in this barbecue sauce. For variety, skewer a bay leaf next to each venison cube for flavor and looks.

- -

1 1/2 # venison, 1" cubes	1 medium onion, chopped	1/2 tsp. Tabasco
12 small tomatoes	3/4 cup beer	
3 green peppers, 1" square	1/4 cup molasses	
4 onions, sectioned	3 tbsp. vinegar	
12 mushrooms	3 tbsp. brandy	
2 tbsp. olive oil	1 1/2 tsp. Worcestershire sauce	
2 cloves garlic, minced	1 (12 oz.) bottle chili sauce	

- -

Alternate venison cubes, tomatoes, pepper squares, mushrooms, and onion sections on 10" skewers. Sauté garlic and chopped onion in olive oil until translucent. Add beer, molasses, vinegar, brandy, Worcestershire sauce, and chili sauce. Simmer until reduced to 2 cups, stir occasionally. Stir in Tabasco sauce. Brush sauce evenly over kabobs. Grill over hot coals adding sauce as needed.

Venison Pablano

Use any large, mild pepper in this Mexican dish. Pablano peppers work especially well because they are very colorful, mild, and large. Dried cranberry and white raisins give this dish an added gourmet touch.

- -

1 # venison steak, 1" thick	2 cloves garlic, minced	Salt & pepper
6 pablano chilies	3 Italian tomatoes, chopped	1 tbsp. basil
8 tbsp. olive oil	1 can tomato soup	1 tbsp. cilantro
1 medium onion, chopped	1/2 can milk	

- -

Fry peppers until they puff up and take on an olive color in 4 tablespoons of hot oil. Peel peppers under cold water. Make a 2" slit in each pepper, remove seeds, and dry thoroughly on towel. Set aside. Sauté garlic and onions in 2 tablespoons oil until onions are translucent. Set aside. Heat tomatoes, milk, tomato soup, basil, salt, and pepper. Brush steaks with remaining 2 tablespoons of oil and broil under direct heat until rare or medium-rare. Keep warm. Slice steak into 1/2" strips. Place 3-4 strips of steak into each pepper. Spoon 2 tablespoons tomato-onion mixture over steak. Spoon tomato soup onto plates and arrange the stuffed peppers on top. Sprinkle with cilantro.

Bacon-Bourbon Cutlets

Grill these tasty cutlets on a very hot grill. The cutlets will be close to rare or medium-rare when the bacon begins to crisp. Venison tenderloins work well here, also.

- -

12 venison cutlets, 1" thick	1 tbsp. soy sauce
6 slices of bacon	1 tbsp. Dijon mustard
3 tbsp. onion, minced	2 green peppers, sectioned
2 tbsp. bourbon	6 cherry tomatoes
1/4 tsp. pepper	2 medium onions, sectioned
2 tbsp. maple syrup	12 tooth picks & 4 (12") skewers

- -

Cut bacon slices in half. Combine the onion, bourbon, pepper, maple syrup, soy sauce, and mustard into a marinade. Let cutlets set in marinade for an hour. Wrap each cutlet with a strip of bacon using a toothpick to hold each slice. Thread cutlets from the side onto skewers along with cherry tomatoes, sections of onion, and green pepper. Grill on very hot grill.

Peppered Cutlets in White Sauce

Broiled cutlets topped with dollops of peppered butter and set in a light white sauce are as attractive as they are delicious. Venison tenderloin is a welcome substitute for cutlets in this recipe.

- -

6 venison cutlets, 1" thick	2 tbsp. butter
1/3 cup soft butter	2 tbsp. flour
1/4 cup chopped red bell pepper	1 cup milk
1/2 tsp. ground red pepper	Salt & pepper
3/4 tsp seasoned salt	1 tbsp. olive oil

- -

Combine 1/3 cup butter, bell pepper, ground pepper, and seasoned salt. Set aside. Heat 2 tablespoons of butter over medium heat in heavy skillet. Add flour, stirring frequently. Slowly add the milk to flour and butter mixture, stirring constantly to eliminate lumps. Add salt and pepper to taste. Brush cutlets with olive oil and broil to medium-rare. Spoon white sauce onto plate or platter. Add cutlets. Top each cutlet with a dollop of butter-pepper mix.

Broiled Venison on a Biscuit

This recipe makes a wonderful breakfast treat next to poached eggs. Or, serve as a hearty hot venison sandwich for dinner smothered in brown gravy alongside mashed potatoes.

- -

2 venison steaks, 1 1/2" thick   1 tsp. dry mustard
1 cup Italian salad dressing   1/4 tsp. lemon-pepper seasoning
2 cloves garlic, minced   6 biscuits
1/3 cup sliced green onions   Coarse grained Dijon mustard
1/2 cup red wine

- -

Combine dressing, garlic, onion, wine, mustard, and seasoning in a bowl or plastic bag. Add steaks, turning to coat. Cover dish or seal bag and refrigerate for 8 hours, or overnight, turning steaks occasionally. Remove steaks and discard marinade. Broil streaks 3" from coals or flame for 2-3 minutes until rare or medium-rare. Thinly slice steaks diagonally across grain. Serve with biscuits and coarse grained mustard.

Sauerkraut Ribs

The combination of sweet barbecue sauce and sour sauerkraut makes this recipe truly delightful. This recipe works especially well in reducing tallow on whitetail ribs.

- -

3 # venison ribs	1/3 cup water
2 cups water	1 tbsp. dry mustard
2 cans beer	1 (12 oz.) bottle chili sauce
1 (14 oz.) bottle ketchup	1 (30 oz.) can sauerkraut
1/2 cup brown sugar	

- -

Trim ribs of as much fat as possible. Put ribs and 2 cups water into a covered roasting pan and bake for 2 hours at 350°. Remove from oven and drain. Add beer and return to oven for another hour or until meat begins to fall from the bones. Drain the ribs once again. Prepare the red sauce by simmering the ketchup, brown sugar, 1/3 cup water, dry mustard, and chili sauce for 10 minutes. Drain the sauerkraut. Combine sauerkraut and red sauce. Heat and pour over ribs. Serve very hot.

Venison Stir-Fry

The combination of venison cutlet, pepper, and artichoke on rice provides a quick, colorful, and tasty entrée. Serve this stir-fry immediately over hot rice.

- -

1/2 # steak	1 tbsp. cornstarch
2 tbsp. olive oil	1 tsp. sugar
1 (14 oz). can artichoke hearts	1/2 tsp. black pepper
2 cups sliced mushrooms	1/4 cup beef bouillon
1/2 cup red pepper, sliced thin	2 cups cooked brown rice
1/2 cup green pepper, sliced thin	

- -

Cut steak into thin slices, 1/4" thick. Heat 1 tablespoon oil in heavy skillet on high heat. Add artichokes, mushrooms, peppers, and garlic. Stir-fry 5 minutes. Set aside. Heat final tablespoon oil to hot, add venison, stir-fry 2 minutes. Remove venison. Dissolve cornstarch in water. Add cornstarch, sugar, beef bouillon, and pepper to skillet. Cook 1 minute or until sauce thickens. Add vegetables and venison.

Venison Tenderloin With Glazed Garlic

Whitetail tenderloins are very fragile (see p.5). Cooked too long, over high heat will destroy the unique characteristics of both tenderloin and garlic; if necessary, substitute venison backstrap for the tenderloin.

- -

1 # venison tenderloin	2 tbsp. maple syrup
6 large cloves minced garlic	2 tbsp. apple cider
Water	2 tbsp. dry champagne
2 tbsp. olive oil	1 1/2 tbsp. chopped onion
Salt & pepper	1 1/2 tbsp. chopped chives

- -

Boil garlic in water for 10 seconds. Drain. Repeat with fresh water then set aside. Melt oil in heavy skillet over high heat. Slice tenderloin into 3/8" cubes. Season with salt and pepper and sauté until slightly brown, about 1–2 minutes. Transfer to platter, cover, keep warm. Add garlic, syrup, and cider to skillet. Simmer until reduced to thickness that will glaze a spoon. Add champagne, onion, and half the chives. Simmer to sauce consistency. Season, pour over meat, and sprinkle with remaining chives.

Venison Tenderloin Compote

Venison tenderloins (see p.5) are only 1" to 1 1/2" wide and about 8" long in whitetail deer. They must be cooked quickly to preserve their tender, juicy qualities. The sugar in this recipe helps cut the sharpness of the cranberry; if necessary, substitute venison backstrap for the tenderloin.

- -

2 whitetail tenderloin (about 1#)	1 tsp. minced orange peel
3 tbsp. water	1/2 tsp. ginger
1/3 cup cranberries	1 1/2 tbsp. olive oil
3 tbsp. orange juice	Salt & pepper
1 tbsp. brandy	1 chopped green onion
1 tbsp. sugar	

- -

Combine water and cranberries. Bring to boil. Remove from heat and let stand for 10 minutes. Add and stir to blend orange juice, brandy, sugar, orange peel, and ginger. Melt olive oil in heavy skillet over medium-high heat. Slice tenderloins to 1" cubes. Season with salt and pepper, then sauté until slightly brown, about 1-2 minutes. Remove meat. Add cranberry mixture to skillet and cook until mixture thickens. Add onions, heat, and spoon over venison.

Sweet & Sour Elk

Sweet and sour recipes are very popular with venison lovers in the U.S. especially in the southwest with elk, mule deer, and antelope. They are also popular in Alaska, Nova Scotia, and Newfoundland with caribou and moose.

- -

1 1/2# elk	1 tbsp. cider vinegar
1 envelope onion soup mix	1 tsp. salt
1/4 cup water or stock	1/4 tsp. pepper
1 (12 oz). jar apricot preserves	2 cups cooked rice (optional)
1/2 cup Russian or Catalina salad dressing	1/4 cup brown sugar

- -

Combine soup mix and water. Let stand for 15 minutes. Add preserves, salad dressing, brown sugar, and vinegar. Mix well. Place elk in a greased cake pan. Sprinkle with salt and pepper. Pour apricot mixture over the elk. Cover and bake at 350° for 45 minutes. Uncover and bake 30 to 40 minutes longer or until meat is fork-tender. Serve over rice.

Oriental Venison Cutlets

Serve this great recipe with individual wedges of buttered, boiled cabbage and a side dish of white or brown rice.

- -

8 venison cutlets	1 tbsp. sesame oil
1 tbsp. olive oil	2 cloves chopped garlic
1/2 tsp. chopped basil	1 tbsp. chopped onion
1/2 tbsp. cervil	1 tbsp. grated ginger
1/2 tbsp. cilantro	1 tbsp. soy sauce
1/2 tbsp. mint	3/4 cup venison or beef stock (see p.179)
1/2 tbsp. parsley	1/2 tbsp. butter

- -

Heat olive oil over medium-high heat in a heavy skillet. Pan-fry cutlets quickly to desired doneness, about 2 mintues on a side. Remove from pan and keep warm. Mix basil, chervil, cilantro, mint, and parsley. Coat each cutlet with sesame oil and herb mix. Add garlic, onion, ginger, soy sauce, and venison stock to pan juices. Simmer about 8 minutes. Swirl in butter and return to simmer. Arrange cutlets on platter or plates and cover with sauce. Serve immediately.

Venison With Green Peppercorns

Slow cooking the whiskey-soaked peppercorns brings out their complex fragrance. Serve with a side dish of buttered noodles, sliced cucumbers, and tomatoes.

- -

1 # venison loin	1 small onion, chopped
1 ounce bourbon whiskey	1/4 cup red wine
1/2 tbsp. green peppercorns	1/4 cup heavy cream
1 tbsp. butter	1/2 tbsp. chives
Salt & pepper	1/2 tbsp. parsley or thyme

- -

Soak green peppercorns in whiskey. Heat olive oil over medium-high heat in a heavy skillet. Salt and pepper loin on both sides. Pan-fry loin about 1 minute then roll slowly until all sides are brown and inside temperature is 135°. Remove from pan and keep warm. Sauté chopped onion. Add peppercorns and whiskey to skillet and simmer for 1 minute. Add wine and cook down to a near glaze, being careful not to burn. After pan cools, add heavy cream and simmer on low heat for 1 minute. Add herbs and any meat juices. Slice roast and cover with hot sauce.

Venison Primavera

Primavera means "spring style," a culinary reference to the use of fresh vegetables as a garnish. So, enhance this popular Italian dish with the addition of
tender chunks of large, crisp vegetables.

- -

1 # venison, 1" cubes	2 cups spagetti sauce
1 large onion	3 cups boiled Rotini pasta
1 green pepper	6 cherry tomatoes
1 cup Italian dressing	Parmesan cheese
6-8 large mushroom caps	

- -

Section onion into large 1" wedges and green pepper into 1" squares. Combine the venison,
onion wedges, and green pepper squares with the Italian dressing. Marinate for 8 hours. When
ready to serve, heat spaghetti sauce with Rotini pasta. Stir-fry venison, onion, green pepper,
tomatoes, and mushrooms with marinade in a hot skillet for about 2 minutes. Pour over pasta
and sprinkle with Parmesan cheese.

Venison Holstein

Sauté or deep-fry the breaded cutlets in this Viennese veal recipe. Either fried or poached eggs are appropriate with this recipe that will serve eight. The rolled anchovies add a nice touch to this dish.

- -

1 1/2 # venison cultets	2 tbsp. olive oil
1 slightly beatened egg	2 tbsp. butter
3 tbsp. milk	Salt and pepper
1/4 cup flour	Lemon slices
1/2 cup Saltine cracker crumbs	Rolled anchovies
or breadcrumbs	Poached eggs for eight

- -

Slice venison cutlets to 1/2" thick then pound to 1/4" thick. Combine beatened egg and milk. Dip cutlets in flour, then in egg/milk wash, then in breadcrumbs. Set aside for at least 15 minutes. Sauté cutlets over medium-high heat for 1-2 minutes per side or until golden brown. Serve with lemon slices and rolled anchovies alongside poached eggs.

> Some folks cover the cooked cutlets with sautéed onions in 1/4 cup beef stock combined with 1/2 cup sour cream.

Chicken-Fried Venison

This recipe is a take-off on that southern dish, Chicken-Fried Steak, that was first served to the author with caribou steak as a substitute for beef. Four hungry hunters devoured the caribou along with mounds of mashed potatoes, gravy, green peas, and buttered roles.

- -

1 1/2 # venison steak, 1/2" thick	1/4 tsp. cayenne
2 tbsp. flour	1/4 tsp. cinnamon
1/2 tsp. salt & 1/4 tsp. pepper	1/2 tsp. ginger
2 tbsp. olive oil	3 tbsp. soy sauce
3 stalks celery, 1 1/2" long	6 green onions, chopped
1 cup mushrooms	

- -

Combine flour, salt, and pepper. Pound the seasoned flour into meat. Meat should end up 1/4" thick. Heat olive oil in heavy skillet over medium-high heat and brown meat on both sides. Combine celery, mushrooms, 2/3 green onions, cayenne, cinnamon, ginger, and soy sauce. Pour over meat. Bring skillet to simmer, cover and cook for 1 hour or until meat is very tender. Cover with remaining green onions and serve hot.

Venison Tournedos

Venison Tournedos are steaks cut from the filet mignon of beef. With venison, this cut is referred to as tenderloin located in the body cavity, along the backbone, just in front of the back legs. On whitetail, tournedos refer to the larger cutlets from the backstrap.

Tournedos With Blue Cheese Butter

In food processor, combine 3 ounces of blue cheese, 5 tbsp. butter, 1 clove garlic, 3 juniper berries, and a touch of hot sauce. Chill.

Cook 2" tournedos to medium rare. Butterfly tournedos, leaving 1/2" "hinge."

Stuff with cheese butter, salt & pepper, and garnish with chives.

LEFTOVERS & GROUND VENISON

This chapter includes recipes for ground, cubed, and shredded venison. Use fresh ground venison in chili, meatballs, and meatloaf or any recipe that calls for ground beef. Use cubed venison for stews, potpies, and pasties. Use shredded venison in tacos, enchiladas, as "barbecued beef," or in tasty sauces.

After trimmed of their larger cuts, a neck roast, the shoulder girdle, backbone, and pelvic girdle are good sources of shredded venison. Often discarded after trimming, each provides a surprising amount of scraps that—being close to the bone—are exceptionally juicy and flavorful. A simple method of removing these tidbits is to roast the bones in a little water or wine along with an envelope of dry onion soup mix until the meat falls from the bones. Once the meat is removed, the bones should be dry roasted until brown then covered with water and simmered slowly to transmit their rich flavors into venison broth (see p.179)

Also, one can recycle leftovers into stews, casseroles, and soups. Even meats used in stockpots or soups—where much of their nutrients and flavor have been lost—are enhanced with the addition of vegetables, spicy sauces, or mustards. Those of us who served in the armed forces will long remember chipped beef on toast, a too-common entrée at breakfast. This recycling is also a common practice with restaurants that convert leftover roast, prime rib, and other cuts into soups, potpies, hash, and pasties.

Quenelles

Quenelles or forcemeats, are small balls of fowl, fish, or meat nicely rolled and used as a garnish for sauces, often adding to the taste and beauty of a dish.

Venison Quenelles

1/4 # venison	1 bay leaf
1/4 # raw ham	Pinch of parsley
Salt & pepper	Pinch of nutmeg

Mince venison and ham very fine in food processor. Add salt, pepper, and spices. Let rest for several hours. Form into little balls about the size of a pecan. Roll in flour and parboil in stock or water. Freeze or refrigerate. Add to hot sauce 5 minutes before serving.

Venison Chili

There must be a million recipes for chili, all of them good at deer camp. This favorite recipe comes from my son-in-law, his annual contribution to the Super Bowl party with the boys.

- -

2 # ground venison	1 1/2 cup chili powder
2 tbsp. olive oil	2 (16 oz.) cans kidney beans
1 large onion, chopped	2 (16 oz.) cans chopped tomatoes
1/4 cup diced green pepper	2 tbsp. chopped jalapeno peppers
1 tbsp. garlic powder	1 tbsp. onion powder
1 tbsp. salt	12 oz. can of beer
48 oz. water	

- -

Brown the venison in olive oil, drain, and set aside. Add onion and green pepper to a large pot and sauté until tender. Combine all ingredients (except beer) in large pot. Bring to boil, stirring occasionally. Add beer and simmer for 1 hour.

Venison Cheese Pie

Venison cheese pie is a wonderful, quick and easy dish that can be prepared ahead of time and frozen. It works well for breakfast, lunch, dinner, or as an appetizer if prepared as mini pies in small tort pans.

- -

1 # ground venison	2 eggs
1 tbsp. olive oil	1 cup cottage cheese
1 large onion, chopped	1 1/4 cup gravy
1 pastry shell	1 package brown gravy
Pepper to taste	

- -

Brown the venison and onion in olive oil. Drain and place in pastry shell. Mix two eggs with cottage cheese. Add gravy to meat and onion. Top with cottage cheese mix. Pepper to taste. Bake 1 hour at 350° or until top is brown.

Venison Egg Rolls

Egg rolls make wonderful appetizers for home or deer camp. Serve with side dishes of sweet and sour sauce, mild and hot mustard. Egg roll dough is available at most large food markets

----

1 1/2 ground venison
2 tbsp. olive oil
2 cloves minced garlic
2 tbsp. peanut butter
Salt & pepper
1 tbsp. Worcestershire sauce

1 can bean sprouts
1 small head cabbage
1 medium onion, chopped
1 package egg roll dough
Cooking oil

Brown venison in olive oil. Drain bean sprouts. Shred cabbage, cover with water, bring to boil, and cook for 10 minutes. Drain well. Combine venison, Worcestershire sauce, garlic, peanut butter, salt and pepper, bean sprouts, and cabbage. Place 1 tablespoon of mix on each square of egg roll dough. Wrap as for egg rolls. Deep-fry until golden brown. Cooking oil should be very hot but not smoking.

French Venison Au Gratin

Use cubed, sliced, or ground venison for these individual casseroles. If
sliced, take care not to overcook. Sharp cheddar in place of the Parmesan
and mozzarella cheese also works.

- -

1 # cubed venison	1 tsp. salt
2 tbsp. olive oil	1/2 tsp. pepper
4 cups sliced onion	4 cups venison borth or beef broth (see p.179)
3 tbsp. flour	2 cups cooked fettucine
1 tbsp. brown sugar	1/2 cup Parmesan cheese
1 tsp. cumin	1 cup shredded mozzarella cheese

- -

Sauté onion in olive oil, stirring until caramelized but not burned. Remove onion, set aside.
Add venison to pan, brown lightly then remove to onion platter. Add broth to skillet. Mix
flour, sugar, cumin, salt, and pepper. Add onion, venison, and flour mix to broth, stir and
simmer 10 minutes. Heat oven broiler. Place 1/2 cup fettucine in oven-proof bowls. Divide
meat mixture over pasta. Mix cheeses together and sprinkle evenly over venison. Broil until
cheese melts and is lightly browned.

8 Little Cheese Loafs

Make these mini-meat loaves 4" long and 2" wide. Serve with spaghetti, a red sauce, and hot garlic bread. Wrapped in venison or pig caul gives these small loafs a gourmet touch.

- -

2 # ground venison
2 beaten eggs
3/4 cup cracker or breadcrumbs
1/2 cup milk
1/2 cup Parmesan cheese
1/4 cup minced onion

1 tbsp. Worcestershire sauce
1 clove minced garlic
1 tsp. Italian seasoning
1/4 cup ketchup or barbecue sauce
3 tbsp. Parmesan cheese

- -

Combine venison, eggs, crumbs, milk, 1/2 cup Parmesan cheese, onion, Worcestershire sauce, garlic, and Italian seasoning. Mix well. Shape into 2" X 4" oval logs. Spread with ketchup and sprinkle with 3 tablespoons Parmesan cheese. Bake at 350° until no pink remains.

Wisconsin Venison Loaf

Lack of venison fat will never be noticed in this hearty meat loaf that offers pockets of moist cheddar cheese with crunchy nuggets of rice. This recipes also works very well as a loaf wrapped in caul (see p.4) and smoked slowly until inside temperature reaches 160°.

1 # ground venison	1 1/4 tsp. salt
2 cups cooked brown rice	2 beaten eggs
2 cups cheddar cheese	3/4 tsp pepper
1 cup breadcrumbs	1 tsp. ground sage
1 cup minced onion	3 tbsp. ketchup
1/2 cup flour	

Combine all ingredients in large bowl. Mix well. Press firmly into a greased bread pan. Spead with ketchup and bake, uncovered at 350° for 1 hour or until no pink remains. A nice glaze in place of ketchup is made by combining 1/4 cup brown sugar with 3 tablespoons cider vinegar, 3 tablespoons of ketchup and 1 tablespoon of prepared mustard. Place glaze on 15 minutes before removing from the oven.

Barbecue Neck Burger

A venison neck roast provides some superb shredded meat for burgers, barbecue beef recipes or any number of Mexican dishes that call for shredded beef (see p.88 for shredding information). A great sandwich is made with shredded barbecued venison neck, caramelized onions, and chopped green olives.

- -

2-3 # venison neck roast
1 cup water or white wine
2 tsp. salt
1 envelope onion soup mix
2 cups ketchup
2 cups diced celery

1/3 cup steak sauce
1/4 cup brown sugar
1/4 cup vinegar
2 tsp. lemon juice
Hamburger buns

- -

Trim fat, tendons, and windpipe from roast. Place roast, water, salt, and soup mix in roasting pan. Cook at 350° for 2 1/2 hours or until meat is tender and falls from the bone. Remove, cool and shred with a fork. Skim fat from cooking liquid and drain all but 1 cup. Add meat, ketchup, celery, steak sauce, brown sugar, vinegar, and lemon juice. Cover and cook over medium-low heat for 1 hour. Serve on toasted buns.

Sweet 'n Sour Meatballs

This recipe comes from a close friend in Chatham Michigan who cans venison as well as she cooks it. The breadcrumbs act as binder and help produce a light, soft meatball. The author noticed many similar recipes in popular cookbooks while hunting caribou and moose in Newfoundland.

- -

2 # ground venison	3 cloves minced garlic
1 # ground pork	2 tbsp. olive oil
1/2 cup milk	<u>Sauce</u>
3 cups soft breadcrumbs	1 (12 oz.) bottle chili sauce
3 eggs	1 (18 oz.) jar grape jelly
Salt & pepper	1/4 cup lemon juice
6 tbsp. minced onion	3 tbsp. horseradish

- -

Soak breadcrumbs in milk. Add venison, pork, eggs, salt, pepper, onion, and garlic. Form into 1 1/2" meatballs. Heat olive oil in heavy skillet to medium-hot. Brown meatballs on all sides. Cover, cook over low heat for 4 minutes. Combine chili sauce, grape jelly, lemon juice, and horseradish. Pour over meatballs. Simmer for 10-12 munutes until sauce thickens.

Venison Goulash

Goulash is a Hungarian dish made in a variety of ways. Beef and veal are sometimes added along with any number of vegetables during the last stage of cooking. As a rule, goulash is heavily spiced with Hungarian paprika.

- -

1 1/2 # ground venison
1 tbsp. bacon drippings
2 large onions, chopped
Salt & pepper
1/2 tsp. cracked peppercorns
1 tbsp. Hungarian paprika

1/2 tsp. thyme
1 (15 oz.) can tomatoes
3 tbsp. tomato sauce
2 cups cooked elbow macaroni

- -

Heat bacon drippings in heavy skillet to medium-hot. Add onion. Sauté until translucent. Brown venison with onions. Reduce heat. Add salt, pepper, thyme, tomatoes, and tomato sauce. Cover and simmer for 30 minutes. Add macaroni. Cover and simmer for 20 minutes.

Venison stock, with its high gelatin content along with the meat scraped from boiled bones, makes a wonderful goulash base.

Bagna Cauda Venison Dip

Bagna Cauda is an Italian anchovy sauce popular during lent, when it was served on Fridays as a dip for fresh vegetables. Southern Italian friends use it as a hot broth to cook vegetables and meat. Here, individual wedges of cabbage leaves are used as "spoons" to gather and eat the hot meat with the sauce.

- -

1 # leftover venison steak or loin

1/2 cup butter

1 can anchovies

1 clove minced garlic

1 tbsp. sugar

1 tbsp. vinegar

1 cup whipping cream

1/2 head cabbage, cut in wedges
1 1/2" wide at the center

- -

Chop steak into small pieces. Heat butter in heavy skillet. Add anchovies and mash with fork until fish dissolves. Add the venison, garlic, sugar, and vinegar. Stir and simmer for 5 minutes. Remove from heat and stir in the whipping cream. Pour sauce into individual serving bowls. Use single pieces of cabbage leaves as "spoons" to eat the venison dip.

Venison Pasty

Venison pasty can be made with only venison or a combination of venison and pork. If only venison is used, add a tablespoon of butter to the meat/vegetable mixture before enclosing in a crust. While carrots are optional here, a little adds color.

- -

1 # ground venison	1/2 cup carrots (optional)
1 # ground pork	1/4 cup parsley
6 # cubed potatoes	Salt & pepper
1 # cubed onions	1/2 cup milk
1 cup cubed rutabaga	10-15 prepared pie crusts

> To save time at camp, put all ingredients in cake pan and cover with biscuit mix.

- -

Mix meat, potatoes, onions, rutabaga, carrots, parsley, salt, and pepper. Place 1 cup of mix 2" off center on a pie crust. Fold large side of dough over the mix. Trim excess dough, leaving 1/2" to crimp with a fork or finger curl. Follow the same procedure with remaining mixture and pie dough. Brush pasty with milk and bake at 350° for 1 hour or until brown and inside temperature is 180°.

Venison Pork Pie

Close friends treat the author, his wife, and many other friends and relative to a Christmas gift of venison-pork pie each and every year. They were also kind enough to share the following recipe that's sufficient for 3 pies.

- -

2 # venison	2 cups water
2 # pork	4 tsp. salt
3 medium potatoes, cubed	4 tsp. pepper
3 medium onions, cubed	1 tsp. allspice
	3 prepared pie crusts

- -

Grind meat, potatoes, and onions through 1/4" plate. Combine meat, potatoes, onions, water, and spices together and simmer for 1 1/2 hours in a heavy skillet, stirring occasionally. Cool and pour off any fat and liquids. Put into pastry-lined pie pans and cover with a top crust. Bake at 450° for 20-25 minutes or until crust is golden brown. Serve with gravy or ketchup.

Venison Stew

Because all the ingredients can be thrown into a pot and left to cook slowly during the afternoon hunt, this is a compulsory recipe for every deer camp. While a can of green peas is optional, lusty grain bread is a must.

- -

2 # venison	4 carrots, 1" cubes
2 stalks celery, 1" cubes	2 tbsp. salt
3 medium potatoes, cubed	4 tsp. pepper
1 tbsp. sugar	4 tsp. tapioka
1 (28 oz.) can diced tomatoes	Heavy grain bread
6 small onions	1 small can of peas (optional)

- -

Combine all ingredients except for peas in heavy pot with good cover. Stir to distribute the spices, sugar, and tapioka evenly. Bake, covered, at 275° for 5 hours checking occasionally to stir and add water if needed. Add peas and serve with bread.

Venison Stew With White Polenta

This tasty stew is guaranteed to satisfy the most demanding appetite. Dollops of biscuit mix are good substitutes for white polenta but should be placed atop the stew 45 minutes before serving to bake and brown.

- -

2 # cubed venison	1 cup chopped tomato	4 cups mushrooms
2 tbsp. olive oil	2 cups cubed carrots	2 tsp. cornstarch
3 cloves minced garlic	2 bay leaves	1 tsp. cool water
2 cups pearl onions	2 cups red wine	
1/4 cup parsley	1 cup venison or beef stock (see p.179)	
1/2 tsp. basil	1/2 cup parsley & 1/2 cup Parmesan cheese	
Salt & pepper	2 cups cooked white polenta	

- -

Brown meat and garlic in oil. In a crock pot, add meat, garlic, carrots, onions, parsley, basil, salt, pepper, wine, tomato, stock, and bay leaves. Heat to boiling then reduce to simmer. Add mushrooms. Combine cornstarch and cold water, heat and stir for 2 minutes. Add to stock and simmer for 45 minutes. Serve in bowls topped with a dollop of hot white polenta, sprinkles of parsley, and Parmesan cheese.

Burgundy Venison

Burgundy venison is a quick and easy dinner certain to clear the camp refrigerator and breadbox of those inevitable leftovers. Any red, white or combination of leftover wine will suffice.

- -

2 # cubed venison	1 can cream of mushroom soup
1/2 cup burgundy wine	1 can cream of chicken soup
1 package of onion soup mix	Salt & pepper
1 can of cream of celery soup	Leftover vegetables
	Toasted leftover bread

- -

Mix venison, burgundy, and soups together. Stir well. Do not add any water. Add salt and pepper to taste. Add any leftover vegetables. Cover and bake at 325° for 2 hours. Stir frequently. Serve over toasted slices of buttered bread.

Hunter Venison

This hunters' recipe was adapted from an old Creole cookbook. The ham and lemon juice give an added burst of flavor to this old classic. Serve with baked sweet potatoes and buttered beans.

----

3 # venison, cubed	1 cup dry white wine
1 tbsp. flour	3 cups venison stock or beef stock (see p.179)
3 tbsp. olive oil	1/2 cup mushrooms
1 small onion, chopped	Zest of one lemon or 1 tbsp. lemon juice
1/4 # minced ham	Salt & pepper
1 clove minced garlic	2 cups croutons
2 bay leaves	1/4 tsp. thyme

Flour venison well then brown with chopped onion in 2 tablespoons of oil. Lower heat and stir in ham, garlic, bay leaves, and thyme. Simmer for 2 minutes. Add wine and simmer for 5 minutes. Add stock and simmer for 1 hour. Add mushrooms and lemon zest. Season to taste. Simmer again for 1/2 hour. Serve hot, topped with croutons.

Venison Stroganoff

Stroganoff is a classic recipe that's generally served with noodles. It's also a tradition in many northern communities that put on game dinners for hunters. To prevent curdling, do not boil the sauce after adding the sour cream.

- -

1 1/2 # venison steak	Salt & pepper
2 tbsp. flour	1/2 tsp. basil
3 tbsp. olive oil	1/4 tsp. nutmeg
3/4 tbsp. chopped onion	1/4 cup sherry or sweet red wine
1/2 cup mushrooms	1 cup sour cream
2 cloves minced garlic	2 cups cooked noodles

- -

Pound the steak to 1/2" thick then cut into 1/2" strips and flour. In heavy skillet, brown venison and chopped onion quickly in 2 tablespoons olive oil. Remove venison and onions. Add remaining oil and sauté the mushrooms and garlic on low heat for 2 minutes. Return venison and onion, add salt, pepper, basil, nutmeg, and wine. Cook for 20 minutes. Remove from heat and stir in the sour cream. Serve over hot noodles.

Hunters Breakfast

Dill pickles have a long European history of being served at breakfast, lunch, dinner, or with appetizers. The combination of dill pickle and spicy sauce makes this southern dish a sure mover for breakfast at any deer camp.

1 # leftover venison	Salt & pepper
2 tbsp. butter	1 tbsp. flour
3 large onions, chopped	1/2 cup stock
1 clove minced garlic	2 dill pickles
1/8 tsp. thyme	2 slices of toast
1 ground bay leaf	2 hard-boiled eggs, halved
1/4 tsp. cayenne	

Slice the leftover venison into thin strips. Sauté the onions in butter to a golden brown. Add garlic, thyme, ground bay leaf, salt, and pepper. Simmer slowly for 10 minutes. Add flour, stock, and pickles sliced very thin. Simmer for 10-15 minutes, stirring occasionally. Add the sliced venison and bake for 20 minutes at 350°. Serve hot over buttered toast with eggs to the side.

Venison Hash on Toast

Excellent flavor and easy preparation are the keys to this classic deer camp breakfast. The traditional recipe calls for corned beef or corned venison (see p.184) but any leftover venison will work.

- -

1 # leftover venison	1/2 cup sweet red wine
4 tbsp. butter	Salt & pepper
1 large onion, chopped	Dash of mustard and vinegar
2 potatoes	2 slices of toast
1 tbsp. flour	2 hard-boiled or poached eggs

- -

Boil potatoes until firm but not soft. Dice and brown in 2 tablespoons of butter. Remove from pan. Chop the leftover venison into bite-size pieces. Sauté the onion to golden brown in 2 tablespoons of butter. Dust onions with flour, add the potatoes, venison, and wine. Simmer until wine is reduced then add dash of mustard and vinegar. Salt and pepper to taste. Quarter hard-boiled eggs. Serve immediately over the toast with eggs on the side.

Venison Mincemeat

Mincemeat pie is more a holiday fare than camp fare but both occasions should warrant this timeless treat. The mincemeat may be made ahead of time and stored refrigerated for several days; don't forget the ice cream when hot and ready to serve.

- -

1 # ground venison	1 cup brown sugar	2 tsp. cinnamon
1/4 # ground beef suet	4 oz. chopped citron	1 1/2 tsp. nutmeg
2 cups raisins	1/3 cup vinegar	1 tsp each salt, cloves, mace,
1 cup currants	1/2 cup slivered almonds	and allspice
1 cup apple cider	Zest of 2 oranges	3 tbsp. brandy
		2 prepared pie crusts

- -

Heat oven to 425°. Mix well all ingredients, except brandy, in large stock pot. Heat to boiling then reduce heat and simmer for 1 hour. Cool and stir in brandy. Fit one pie crust into 9-inch pie plate. Fill with mincemeat. Cover with remaining pie crust. Seal and crimp edges. Cut several holes for steam to escape. Brush with milk and bake until crust is golden brown.

Venison Pizza

A Newfoundland guide shared this pizza recipe that he prepared with ground moose. Since then, the author has made the recipe with thin, yeast pizza dough in place of pie crusts. Both crusts worked well.

- -

1 # ground venison	1 tsp. salt
2 tbsp. melted butter	1/2 tsp. pepper
1/2 cup potato flakes	1/4 cup ketchup
1 beaten egg	1 tbsp. mustard
1/4 cup hamburger relish	1/2 cup chopped onions
1/2 cup shredded cheddar cheese	2 prepared pie crusts

- -

Combine 1/4 cup potato flakes and melted butter. Set aside. Combine all other ingredients except pie crusts. Mix well. Roll one pie crust into a circle large enough to cover a greased pizza pan. Spread meat filling over crust. Roll out remaining dough and place on top of filling, sealing edges. Brush with milk and sprinkle with buttered potato flakes. Cut several holes for steam to escape. Bake at 375° for 20 minutes or until golden brown.

Upside-Down Pie

Upside-Down Pie offers the camp chef an opportunity to present old camp dishes in a more interesting fashion. Any number of vegetables (sliced pepper rings, a sprinkle of chives, or shaved green onions) may be used to garnish the top before serving.

1 # ground venison	1 tsp. salt
2 tbsp. olive oil	1/2 tsp. pepper
1/4 cup chopped green pepper	1 tsp. mustard
1/2 cup chopped celery	1 1/2 cup biscuit mix
1/2 cup chopped onion	1/3 cup water
1 can tomato soup, undiluted	3 slices processed cheese, halved diagonally

Heat oil in heavy skillet. Add venison, pepper, celery, and onion; simmer until meat is no longer pink and vegetables are tender. Add the soup, salt, pepper, and mustard. Mix well and transfer to pie plate. Combine the baking mix and water. Roll into 9" circle and place over mix. Bake at 425° for 20 minutes or until golden brown. Cool for 5 minutes. Run a knife around the pie plate to loosen biscuit, then invert onto serving platter. Arrange cheese slices nicely on top, slice, and serve.

ORGANS & BONES

Off cuts of meat from the carcass have been both enjoyed and ignored for centuries. For those who consider such delicacies as marrow, liver, tongue, kidney, heart, lungs (generally referred to as "lights"), and brain a treat, the antlered family offers a wide variety of shapes and sizes to choose from.

Venison heart and liver make excellent entrees, pickles, and pâtés. Heart has a smooth, soft texture and a mild taste that appreciates a good sauce or marinade. Regardless of the recipe, remove all blood vessels leading to and from the heart as well as all connective tissue within the four chambers. A healthy liver is purple-pink. Discard any liver with off-colored yellow or gray spots. Before cooking, rinse in cold water to remove any foreign particles then cut away all fatty tissue, connective tissue, large blood vessels, and ducts. Livers taken from adult animals should also be skinned. This is best done by first cutting the liver into half-inch slices then trimming the skin from around the edge. Liver is best cooked fresh and not overcooked. It's done when pink blood oozing out runs clear.

Most will find venison tongue a pleasant surprise, as good as any beef tongue. Elk, moose, and caribou tongue are large and, therefore, easy to process. Whitetail and antelope tongue only present a problem because of their size but both are tasty and flavorful. A tongue is generally soaked in a salt solution for an hour then blanched for 15 minutes followed by submersion in ice water before removing the skin. Some recipes may call for a presoak in wine, vinegar, lemon juice, buttermilk, or a combination of these liquids before cooking. Once skinned, it may be smoked or pickled, corned or canned, dry cured, or used in a gelatin loaf, like headcheese.

Size plays a role in locating and processing venison kidneys. Here, again, elk, moose, and caribou kidneys are relatively large, easy to locate, and more simple to process. But, for even a large 150-pound whitetail, the kidneys are small—about three inches long and 2 inches wide—and hidden by large deposits of fat or tallow. They are located along the backbone near the back legs. Regardless, they all benefit from discarding all connective tissue and vessels along with quick blanching in boiling water before use in a recipe.

Usually brains are soaked in cold water—about one hour in salted water—to rid them of excess blood which can give them an off flavor and color. The thick outer membrane is best removed before poaching. Poaching consist of placing the brain in enough salted water to cover and simmering under medium-low heat for 30 minutes followed by cooling in its own liquid. It's important to keep the water at a gentle simmer to prevent the tissue from breaking apart.

Poaching in salted water or beef broth is a favorite way of preparing venison marrow as well as venison brain. For the better part of human history, bone marrow was an important part of our diet as a great source of animal fat so necessary for proper growth. It is still part of the European diet, especially in France. Once poached, it can be used in sauces or soups, as dumplings, or as an entrée. Marrow should always be served hot. If left to cool, it will congeal in an unattractive fashion.

Of all the off cuts, both venison lights and venison marrow are least appreciated. It's only been in the last several years that one can find menus featuring venison marrow. Though not very popular, it's now chic for the more elegant restaurants specializing in wild game to serve a roll of thighbones along with a long, thin spoon to dig out the delicacy. Lights are still added to sauces, soups, pâtés and sausages. Most traditional recipes for haggis and andouilli, for example, call for the use of lights.

Salting Venison Tongue
The flavor of venison tongue is greatly improved with a day of salting before cooking. Salting is carried out by rubbing the tongue with Mortons® Tender Quick® or canning salt. Rotate the tongue in the mixture several times during the day before cooling and skinning.

Heart Jerky
A simple recipe resulting in a "jerky" type product is to boil the heart in salted water for 1/2 hour. Then, slice thin and fry quickly in hot butter or olive oil. Add salt and pepper to taste.

Liver Dumplings

The addition of pig liver here provides for a lighter, softer dumpling. Use a teaspoon dipped in hot soup or water to help shape the dumplings.

- -

1/4 # venison liver	1 tsp. salt
1/4 # pig liver	1/8 tsp. pepper
1 small onion, grated	1/8 tsp. thyme
1 egg	3/4 cup flour
2 tbsp. parsley	3 slices stale bread
1/8 tsp. nutmeg	2 cups soup or gravy
1 cup milk	

- -

Remove tubes and cut liver into 1/2" slices. Trim the skin from the slices. Cover with water and blanch for 3 minutes. Grind the liver and onion through a fine plate or process in food processor. Mix throughly with egg, parsley, nutmeg, salt, pepper, and thyme. Cut the bread into small cubes and soak in milk then squeeze dry. Add the bread and flour to the liver mix and kneed into a stiff paste. Form dumplings into 1" rounds and drop into boiling soup or gravy. Cover and simmer for 10-15 minutes.

Brains With Black Butter

A slight variation on this classic recipe includes the addition of paprika in the seasoned flour and capers to the sauce. Capers add additional texture and a wonderful subtle flavor to this dish.

- -

2 small or 1 large brain	Seasoned flour: 1 cup flour, 1 tsp. salt,
2 tbsp. vinegar	1 tsp. pepper, and 1 tbsp. paprika
1 tsp. salt	3/4 cup butter
1 quart water	2 tbsp. vinegar
3 tbsp. butter	1 tbsp. capers

- -

If present, remove outer membrane. Soak brains in cold water for 1 hour. Bring the vinegar, salt, and water to boil. Submerge brains in vinegar water and simmer slowly for 30 minutes. Remove and plunge in cold water. Let stand until cool. Dry and cut in 1/4"-1/2" cubes, dip into seasoned flour. Sauté in butter at medium-high heat until golden. Remove from pan, cover with capers, and set aside. Heat 3/4 cup butter in sauté pan until it just begins to brown. Remove, add 2 tablespoons of vinegar, stir, and return to heat until sauce begins to foam. Pour sizzling sauce over brains and serve immediately.

Fried Liver And Onion

Fried venison liver and onion was standard fare in hunting camps throughout the United States for decades. Our national concern over cholesterol has moderated this long-held custom but some camps still insist the first liver brought to camp be served in this traditional fashion.

- -

1 # venison liver	Salt & pepper
3 tbsp. flour	1 tbsp. butter
2 tbsp. bacon drippings	2 tbsp. parsley
1 large onion, sliced	1 orange sliced thin
1/2 cup sweet red wine or sherry	

- -

Remove tubes and skin from the liver. Julienne liver into pencil-sized pieces. Pat dry and coat with flour. Sauté liver quickly in hot bacon grease. Liver is done when pink blood oozing out runs clear. Remove from heat. Sauté onions until soft but not brown. Remove to plate with liver. Heat wine in sauté pan, stirring in the brown bits from bottom of pan. Add salt and pepper. Swirl butter into sauce until it just melts. Pour over liver and onions. Garnish with parsley and orange slices.

Venison Liver in Sherry

Sauté the liver and garlic in this recipe with care to elicit the faint nutty flavor of the garlic and maintain the liver's tender texture.

- -

1/2 # liver, cut in 3/8" slices	3 tbsp. beef stock or venison stock (p.179)
4 tbsp. olive oil	Salt & pepper
1 carrot, sliced thin	2 tbsp. of flour
1 bay leaf	2-3 sprigs fresh thyme & several bay leaves
1 clove garlic, sliced thin	1 tomato, skinned & chopped
1 cup sherry or red wine	

- -

Sauté carrots, bay leaf, and garlic in a heavy skillet with 2 tablespoons of olive oil over medium heat. Add wine or sherry. Bring to boil and add stock along with salt and pepper. Cook to 1/2 volume. Set aside. Salt and pepper liver on both sides, then dredge in flour. Sauté liver with remaining oil until blood runs clear. Spread liver on plate. Decorate plate with sprigs of thyme and bay leaf. Reheat sauce in skillet stirring in bits from liver. Pour over liver. Spoon chopped tomato to one side.

Boiled Heart In Piquant Sauce

Piquant sauce is a thick onion sauce containing a blend of spices, vinegar, and pickle. The combination compliments the texture and flavor of venison heart very nicely. An average whitetail heart weighs 1 pound.

- -

1 # venison heart	1/2 tsp. parsley
2 onions, chopped	Cayenne pepper to taste
1 tbsp. olive oil	Salt & pepper
1 tbsp. stock or water	1 tbsp. cider vinegar
2 cloves minced garlic	1 medium dill pickle, sliced thin
1/4 tsp. thyme	1 minced bay leaf

- -

Remove all blood vessels and tough tissue lining inside the heart. Cover heart with salted water and simmer for 1 hour or until a fork penetrates with ease. Cut heart into 3/8" slices and set aside. Brown the onions in olive oil. Add the stock or water, garlic, thyme, parsley, salt, pepper, and cayenne pepper. Add vinegar and thin slices of dill pickle. Simmer for 10 minutes. Serve sauce over the boiled heart.

Baked Heart

Be sure all blood vessels and tough tissue lining inside the heart are removed for this basic recipe. Add two cups of canned tomatoes or venison stock (see p.179) during baking to help keep the moisture content high and to serve as a gravy base. An average whitetail heart weighs 1 pound.

- -

2 # venison heart	1/4 cup butter
1 quart salted water	1 cup finely chopped celery
2 cups cubed bread	1 tsp. sage
1/2 cup milk	2 cups diced tomato or stock
1 large onion, diced	Salt & pepper

- -

Boil hearts in salted water until tender, about 1 hour. Soak bread cubes in milk, then drain. Sauté onion and celery in butter until onion bits are transparent. Add bread, salt, pepper, and sage to onion and celery. Mix well. Split hearts and fill with dressing. Pack rest of dressing around the heart. Add tomato or stock. Bake at 325° for 2 hours or until a fork penetrates heart with ease.

Kidneys In Cream Sauce

Kidneys In Cream Sauce is a favorite family recipe usually done with beef kidneys. The kidney's unique flavor combines with the onion, tomato, wine, and whipping cream to produce a truly memorable dish. Serve with polenta. Eight whitetail kidneys weigh about 1 pound.

----

1 # venison kidney	1 tsp. parsley
3 tbsp. salt	1 cup dry red wine
4 cups water	2 tbsp. tomato paste
2 onions, chopped	1 cup whipping cream
2 tbsp. olive oil	Pepper to taste

Dissolve salt in water, add kidneys and soak overnight. Place kidneys in quart of cold water, heat to boiling, then drain. Repeat the boiling a second time. Cut kidneys into bite-size pieces, trimming away all fat, and tubes. Set aside. Brown onions in oil. Add parsley and garlic. Add kidneys, tomato paste, and wine. Cover and bake for 2 hours at 325°. Remove kidneys. Stir in whipping cream. Retun kidneys to the cream sauce. Serve very warm over polenta.

Venison Haggis

This old recipe remains popular in the British Isles where a sheep's stomach pouch (see p.18) is used for casing and pluck (liver, lungs, and heart) is used as stuffing. Some authors consider haggis a fresh sausage. Haggamuggie is a version of haggis made with fish liver.

- -

1/4 # ground venison	1/4 cup oatmeal
1/4 # venison heart	1 tsp. ginger
1/4 # venison liver	1 tsp. nutmeg
1/4 # beef suet	1 tsp. pepper
	Beef gravy to cover links

- -

Soak oatmeal in water overnight. Keep suet very cold to assist in grinding. Grind meat and suet through smallest plate or chop fine with food processor. Mix meat, suet, oatmeal, and spices well. Stuff into large 40-45 mm beef casings. Make each haggis into separate sausages, about 3" long. Submerge sausages in 180° water until inside temperature reaches 155°. Remove from water and cool in ice water. To serve, simmer in beef broth for about 20 minutes, then brown and serve.

Liver & Raisin Pâté

Liver & Raisin Pâté is a coarse pâté that's simple to create in the microwave. The volume of raisins helps reduce the high cholesterol content while the sweetness helps reduce the sharper liver taste.

- -

1/2 # venison liver slices	3 tbsp. red wine
4 shallots, chopped	1/2 cup breadcrumbs
1 clove garlic, minced	1/4 tsp. salt
1 tbsp. olive oil	1/4 tsp. pepper
1 cup raisins	

- -

Stir shallots, garlic, and oil in bowl. Cover and microwave on high for 3 minutes. Stir at 2 minutes. Add venison liver and red wine. Microwave on high for 5 minutes, stirring at 3 minutes. Cool slightly, then place all ingredients in food processor or blender and process to a coarse pâté. Refrigerate overnight before serving.

Venison Marrow

The following suggestions are for 2 complete whitetail thighbones. Use a very sharp saw to cut the thigh bone into 2"-4" lengths. Then, process using one of the following techniques.

1) Roast in a moderate 350° oven about 1 hour. Marrow will be done when a thin knife or narrow fork penetrates the marrow without resistance. Once roasted, the marrow can be scooped out and spread on pieces of fresh toast. Several roasted bones of different lengths—from 2"-4" long—tied nicely with a ribbon or cord are served as the main entrée in some fancy restaurant. They are served as an upright clump of bones with long thin spoons or knives for scooping and spreading.*

2) Simmer the bones in your favorite soup for about 20 minutes. When the marrow is tender, scoop it out and serve to garnish the soup as marrow quenelles (see p.136).

3) Poach bones in salted water for 10 minutes. Remove marrow. Mix 3 tablespoons of marrow with 2 eggs, 1/2 cup breadcrumbs, 3 tablespoons chopped parsley, salt, pepper, and a teaspoon of lemon juice. Form into small dumpling. Drop into boiling venison or beef stock for about 4 minutes or until they float to surface. Add to brown sauces made from beef or venison broth flavored with a bit of red wine, bay leaf, and thyme.

*Marrow should always be served hot. If left to cool, it will congeal in an unattractive fashion.

Pickled Venison Tongue

Any recipe used to prepare beef tongue can be used to prepare venison tongue. A caribou tongue is about 3 pounds, a moose tongue about 5 pounds and an average whitetail tongue about 3/4 pound.

- -

3 # venison tongue	2 tsp. paprika
2 tbsp. Morton® Tender Quick®	1 tbsp. pickling spices
4 cups water	1/4 cup warm water
3 tbsp. brown sugar	2 bay leaves
2 cloves minced garlic	1 tsp. cloves
	1 small onion

- -

Soak tongue in a salt solution for an hour then blanch for 15 minutes. Next, submerge in ice water and remove the skin. Bring to boil all ingredients, then cool. Pour mixture over venison tongue in a plastic or ceramic bowl. Weigh down tongue with a heavy plate. Marinate for 10 days, turning the meat occasionally. After ten days, remove and soak in lukewarm water for 1 hour. Cover meat with cold water. Bring to a boil and simmer for 1/2 hour. Add bay leaves, onion, and cloves. Simmer gently until meat is tender. Serve warm or hot.

STOCK-PICKLES & CANNED VENISON

Making pickle and stock has become a lost art with the advent of refrigeration. This should not be the case because venison, and its byproducts, are too valuable a resource to waste, including the broth made from venison bones. Plus, a good stock or pickle offers a host of interesting ways to prepare venison. After all, a pickle is nothing more than a vinegar marinade designed to tenderize, flavor, and in some cases preserve. When used to tenderize and flavor, individual tastes are further enhanced with the addition of a favorite spice, a touch of sugar, or a dash of sherry to the pickle.

Pickles and wet cures—also known as brine solutions—are generally used for small cuts of meat. One cup of salt or a salt/sugar mix in eight cups of water is sufficient to cure two or three pounds of meat. A simple check to determine the appropriate ratio of water to cure is to place an egg in the solution. If it sinks, more salt should be added until the egg just breaks the surface. Small cuts can brine in one or two hours. A large three-pound cut may take two or three days for a complete cure. For a ten-pound cut, the typical recipe calls for one pound of salt, a cure—such as Prague Powder #1 or Instacure #1—to 2 1/2 gallons of water.

Venison stock offers similar adventures. Stock is fundamental to good cooking. The large, meaty bones from the neck, back, ribs, and legs spawn a wonderful broth adding as much or more flavor to a recipe than chicken or beef broth. Stock can also be made from a combination of venison bones and pork hocks, venison bones and ham, venison bones and chicken bones, or other combinations of bones as well as a variety of vegetables.

The concept is simple: Roasted and boiled bones, along with their marrow, release flavors and gelatin that—when combined with certain vegetables produce a base liquid for gravies, stews, marinades, and jelly loafs. The thing to remember about making stock is to use only enough water to cover the ingredients so as to concentrate the flavors and gelatin. For storage purposes, or to concentrate flavors, reduce the stock by simmering, uncovered to half volume. Reduced to one-quarter volume usually results in the stock forming a thick gel.

<u>Cooking Tough Cuts of Pickled Venison</u>
After the meat is pickled (p.177), cover with cold water and simmer for 1 hour. Drain, cover with fresh cold water, add **4** bay leaves, 1 tsp. cloves and 1 medium onion. Bring to boil and simmer gently until the meat is tender.

Venison Sauerbraten

Many folks like their sauerbraten "straight," without the ginger snaps and raisins, while others favor traditional fare that includes a serving of potato dumplings.

4 # venison roast	2 tbsp. olive oil
Salt and pepper	1 medium onion, sliced
3 bay leaves	1/4 cup raisins
1 tsp. peppercorns	6 ginger snap cookies
4 cups water	1/4 cup sugar
4 cups vinegar	1 cup sour cream

Sprinkle meat with salt and pepper. Rub in thoroughly. Place venison, bay leaves, and peppercorns in plastic bag or plastic bowl. Combine water and vinegar and pour over meat. Marinate for 8 days in refrigerator. Heat olive oil to hot in heavy skillet and brown meat on all sides. Place meat and onion slices in roasting pan with 1 cup of the marinade. Roast for 3-4 hours or until tender adding more marinade as needed. Strain liquid. Simmer liquid in skillet with sugar, raisins, and ginger snaps until thickened and smooth. Stir in sour cream and pour over meat.

Process Canned Venison

Canning is a great way to handle that excess game when the freezer gets too full. Plus canned venison offers a great source of cooked meat and gravy for that quick meal at camp.

- -

5 # venison, 1" cubes	2 cups water
2 cups soy sauce	2 cups venison or beef stock (p.179)
3/4 cup olive oil	1 tbsp. sugar
2 1/4 tsp. sugar	3/4 cup vinegar
2 tsp. black pepper	Liquid smoke (optional)
4 cloves minced garlic	Canning jars with caps
1 1/2 tsp. Worcestershire sauce	

- -

Combine venison, soy sauce, oil, 2 1/4 tablespoons sugar, pepper, garlic, Worcestershire sauce, liquid smoke, and water in a roasting pan. Cover tightly and bake for 2 hours at 300°. Bring stock, vinegar, and 1 tablespoon sugar to a boil. Pack meat into clean, hot canning jars. Cover with boiling stock broth. Cold pack according to directions.

Venison Jelly Loaf

This is a simple verson of the technique used to produce headcheese. The slow cooking produces a broth that's great in a jelly loaf, as a appetizing sauce, or as the base for a rich gravy. For a quick, tasty stew, add 2 cups of cubed potatoes and 1 cup of peas to the stock pot during the last 30 minutes of cooking. If using whitetail venison, remove all tallow.

- -

1 1/2 # venison with bones	1 large carrot
1/4 # ham	2 cups dry, white wine
1 pork hock	1 cup water
1 medium onion	Salt & pepper

- -

Chop fine the venison, ham, carrot, and onion. Place all ingredients into a stock pot with a good cover. Cook slowly for about 5-6 hours. Strain broth from the vegetables and meat. Trim meat from bones and disgard bones. Allow broth to cool, then skim the fat. Salt and pepper to taste. Reduce broth to 1/3 volume to concentrate the gelatin. Layer the venison, ham, and pork in a bread pan. Cover with warm broth. Refrigerate to set.

Pickled Venison

Many old timers consider pickled venison the quintessential seasoned meat for their favorite rice dish, bean dish, boiled dinner, or breakfast hash. Add varying amounts of brown sugar or cane sugar to cut the dominant vinegar flavor.

2 # venison steak, 1" thick	1/2 tbsp. white sugar
1 quart distilled white vinegar	1 bay leaf
1/2 cup mustard seed	6 cloves minced garlic
2 tbsp. Tabasco sauce	1 tbsp. salt
1 tbsp. brown sugar	12 peppercorns

Combine all ingredients, except the venison, in a non-reactive pot and boil for 3 minutes. Cool, add the venison and refrigerate for 3 days. At this point the venison is pickled and ready to add to a boiled dinner with cabbage, potatoes, and a few carrots. Or it might be browned in butter as a hash—with boiled, cubed potatoes and some fried onions—alongside scrambled eggs.

Venison Stock

Following is a basic recipe for stock made strickly from venison bones. Although leg bones with their thick marrow offer the most flavor, neck and backbones also work well. One or two veal or pork shanks add additional flavor.

- -

5 # venison bones	1 bay leaf
Water to cover bones	10 peppercorns
2 stalks celery	1 tbsp. parsley
2-3 carrots, 1" pieces	1/4 tsp. thyme
1 medium onion quartered	1/2 cup sherry

- -

Roast bones at 400° for one hour, then transfer to a stock pot adding enough water to just cover the bones. Add clery, carrots, onion, bay leaf, peppercorns, parsley, and thyme. Cover and simmer for about 8 hours, then strain. Add sherry. Cook remaining liquid, uncovered, to 1/4 volume. The stock at this point is ready to freeze, can, use as a broth, or be reduce to a thick, rubbery gel for recipes such as headcheese.

> For a richer stock, saw the bones, especially the leg bones in small pieces 2-3 inches long to expose the marrow.

Venison-Pork Loaf

The pickled pork and venison may be prepared days before and refrigerated. The pickle is a bit more complex here but provides a wonderful blend of flavors for the Swiss chard.

- -

1 # venison, 1" thick	1 clove minced garlic	1/2 cup chopped mushrooms
1 # pork steak, 1" thick	6 juniper berries	1 tsp. ground juniper berry
1/2 cup white vinegar	6 black peppercorns	1 clove minced garlic
1 1/2 cup red wine	4 allspice berries	1 tsp. ground allspice
1 small onion sliced	Touch of clove & mace	1 cup cooked, chopped Swiss
	Salt & pepper	chard

- -

Make pickle with vinegar, wine, onion, garlic, juniper and allspice berries, peppercorns, cloves and mace. Bring to boil, cool, add pork and venison. Pickle for about 2 days. Remove from pickle and rince in fresh water. Reserve 1/2 cup pickle. Chop meat into 1/4" squares. Mix well with mushrooms, Swiss chard, 1 clove minced garlic, ground allspice, ground juniper berry, and 1/2 cup pickle. Salt and pepper to taste. Form into loaf and—if available—wrap with venison or pig caul (p.4). Bake at 300° for 1 hour.

Pickled Venison Roast

A small shoulder roast or rump roast pickles well. Remove as much of the silver membrane covering the meat as possible before pickling. With large roasts it may be necessary to divide the roast in half to facilitate pickle absorption.

- -

2-3 # venison roast	10 whole allspice
1/2 cup vinegar	1 bay leaf
1 tbsp. salt	3 cloves minced garlic
3 cups water	1 1/3 cup sour cream
1 large onion, sliced	Zest of 1/2 lemon

- -

Trim venison roast and dust with salt. Combine vinegar, 2 cups water, onion slices, allspice, bay leaf, and garlic in non-reactive container. Cover and boil 15 minutes. Cool, add roast. Marinate for 3 days in a cold place, turning daily. Remove roast and rinse with water. Bake roast at 325° with 1/2 cup marinade, remaining cup of water, and zest of lemon for 30 minutes per pound. Turn roast once and baste frequently. Add sour cream when done and serve with potatoes or dumplings.

Venison Galantine

Galantine is luncheon meat usually made with boned pork or chicken set in gelatin stock. Prepared venison tongue or heart as described in the introduction to this chapter are excellent substitutes for the venison steak suggested below.

- -

1 1/2 # venison steak, 1" thick	6 cups water
2 # chicken with bones	1 bay leaf
8 cups water	6 cloves minced garlic
3/4 cup Morton® Tender Quick®	Pepper to taste
1/4 cup brown sugar	3/4 cup white vinegar

- -

Combine venison, chicken, 8 cups water, salt, Tender Quick®, and sugar in non-reactive pot. Be sure all ingredients are dissolved. Cure for 2 days in cool place, then rinse under fresh water. Combine 6 cups water, meat, bay leaf, and garlic in large stockpot. Cover and simmer for 1 hour. Remove meat—discard bones—and dice into 1/2" pieces. Place in bread pan. Reduce stock to 2 cups. Add pepper and vinegar, stir and pour over meat. Cool thoroughly before attempting to slice.

Newfoundland Canned Venison

Canning venison has a long history mainly because canned venison is so good. Generally, most recipes suggest the meat be cooked ahead of time using a variety of vegetables, liquids, and spices. The meat and liquid is then cold-packed in canning jars. The following Newfoundland recipe simplifies the process. The key is long cooking in the jars.

- -

Cubed venison

Bacon

Salt

Pint canning jars with new seals & caps

Water

- -

Place a heaping teaspoon of bacon at the bottom of each clean canning jar. Pack venison into jars. Place another heaping teaspoon of bacon on top of the venison. Add 1/2 teaspoon of salt. Add 3 tablespoons of water to each jar. Loosely attach caps. Place jars in pot, cover with cold water to neck of jars. Bring to boil, turn down heat to medium and simmer for 3 1/2 hours. Check water to insure water remains at neck level. Remove from pot, tighten cap so cover is firmly sealed. Check jars a week or so later to insure seal is secure.

Corned Venison

Corning is a wet cure process in which small cuts of meat are marinated in a salt/spice brine and then simmered in water. Top or bottom rounds from the hindquarters of whitetail, the brisket, or any 2-3 pound roast from moose, elk, or caribou will work.

- -

2 # venison roast
2 quart cold water
4 tbsp. brown sugar
2 tbsp. pickling spices
3 small bay leaves

1/2 cup salt
2 tsp. garlic
10 juniper berries
1 tbsp. black peppercorns
1/2 cup Tender Quick®

- -

Place spices, salt, Tender Quick®, and water in non-metal pot and heat to boiling. Cool completely. Submerge meat in the brine and refrigerate for 3 days. Rinse meat in cold water. Place meat in pot, cover with fresh water and bring to boil. Simmer for 1 hour. Leave meat in water during cooling. Serve by slicing across grain.

Corned Venison Glaze
2 tbsp. prepared mustard
2 tbsp. brown sugar
1/4 tsp. nutmeg
1/8 tsp. pepper
Mix all ingredients.
Spread on venison. Bake
for 30 minutes at 350°.

Corned Venison Hash

Corned venison hash is a wonderful use of leftover potatoes. Be sure to brown the potatoes before adding the venison which needs only to warm. Gravy, tomato sauce, peppers, pimentos, or most any leftover vegetable may be included.

- -

1 # corned venison (p.184)	1 green bell pepper, chopped
2 1/2 # potatoes	1/2 tsp. salt
2 tbsp. olive oil	1/4 tsp. pepper
1 medium onion, chopped	1/8 tsp. ground nutmeg

- -

Peel and boil potatoes for 15 minutes or until tender. Drain, cool, and cut into 1/4" cubes. Heat oil in heavy skillet over medium-high heat. Add potatoes, onion, and pepper. Cook until potatoes are brown. Reduce temperature, add corned venison and remaining ingredients. Cook, stirring occasionally until venison is heated through.

INDEX
SIDEBARS
AND
NOTES

INDEX by CHAPTER

A GOURMET'S GUIDE TO VENISON SAUSAGE AND COOKING VENISON

A GOURMET'S GUIDE TO VENISON SAUSAGE AND COOKING VENISON

ALPHABETICAL LISTING

A GOURMET'S GUIDE TO VENISON SAUSAGE AND COOKING VENISON

A GOURMET'S GUIDE TO VENISON SAUSAGE AND COOKING VENISON

ORDER FORM

Woodcock Press

Shipping Address

Name_____

Address_____

City_____State_____Zip_____

Phone_____

A Gourmet's Guide to Venison Sausage
and Cooking Venison..............$14.95

Forest Wildlife and Ecology.......$13.95

Dumbing Down Deer Hunting......$9.95

Title	Quantity	Unit Price	Total Price

Subtotal...

Shipping and Handling ($2.50 for the
first book. 50¢ each additional book.......

Total Order Amount...........................

Mail this form with check or money order to Woodcock Press
14636 Chapel Lane, Rock, Michigan 49880